Wybert Reeve

Romance of Reality

Tales From a Wanderer's Diary

Wybert Reeve

Romance of Reality
Tales From a Wanderer's Diary

ISBN/EAN: 9783744675321

Printed in Europe, USA, Canada, Australia, Japan

Cover: Foto ©Thomas Meinert / pixelio.de

More available books at **www.hansebooks.com**

ROMANCE OF REALITY;

OR,

TALES FROM A WANDERER'S DIARY.

Yrs faithfully

Wybert Reeve

ROMANCE OF REALITY;

OR,

TALES FROM A WANDERER'S

DIARY.

BY

WYBERT REEVE,

COMEDIAN.

SHEFFIELD:

PAWSON AND BRAILSFORD, HIGH STREET.

1862.

DEDICATION.

TO CHARLES KEAN, ESQ.

Dear Sir,

In dedicating to you these few cursory sketches, I feel a considerable amount of gratification, that through their means I am enabled publicly to express my admiration for your long and arduous endeavours, during your management of the Princess's, to raise the legitimate Drama of this country from the slough into which it had apparently fallen, dating from the efforts of Mr. Macready at the Theatres Royal, Drury Lane and Covent Garden.

True, it found a home for some years at Sadler's Wells, under the spirited management of Mr. Phelps, but both the locality and dimensions of that theatre rendered it certainly unworthy of being the ONLY shelter left where that grand foundation on which, to a great extent, rests our literary fame, the works of our dramatists could be presented with sufficient power.

To you sir, then, is due the credit of those revivals, by means of which the audience were not only enabled to enjoy and profit by the beautiful poetry of the dramatist, but that very poetry became intensified, by the reality given to it, in restoring the scenes, habits, and dresses of the age depicted, according to the most authentic sources: and as in the "Midsummer Night's Dream," by occasional appeals to the ideal senses, bearing out and illustrating the fervid and imaginative beauty of the great master-mind of the Bard of Avon. By such means, those who never otherwise would have sought for the knowledge became familiar with men and manners of the historic past, and learned to appreciate Shakespeare, who in dying left to England a legacy in his works immortal as those of Homer, Plato, Cicero, Sophocles, or Virgil, names which cast a halo of earthly grandeur and consecrate with undying fame the very ruins of fallen empires.

Cavillers (and they are ever to be found) may term those revivals spectacles: they and we may look back with pride to the achievement of a Betterton, a Macklin, or a Garrick, and we may thank heaven at the same time we are removed from those primitive days when a bag-wig and square-cut coat, with breeches, marred the grandeur of Lear or the glowing philosophy of Hamlet; whilst, in reading the "Stage Directions" to the early editions of Shakespeare, and the list of properties possessed by the Lord Admirals and other companies of the sixteeenth century, we have direct proof, it was the *will* of the poet and the custom of the period to introduce, as far as their rude and primitive appliances furnished them, the pomp of majesty, the uproar of battle, or of the elemental storm into their Dramatic representations.

You, sir, having retired from managerial anxieties, well-wishers to the Drama can only hope some other gentleman will, ere long, be found with sufficient energy, pecuniary resources, and ability to follow in your footsteps and re-create the public taste, recalling it from the present morbid worship of the horrible and a craving after sensations, which are alike to be found in our modern dramas, our gymnastic exhibitions, and our *criminal executions*. Once a more intellectual and human taste could firmly be established, another dawn for the pure English Drama might arise, obscuring and finally banishing that *shadow* of the true art which now hangs over it, and the wretched effusions, frequently of French parentage, now, in too many instances, finding a place on the London boards, in the shape of Play, Comedy, or Farce, would be abolished, giving place to a more moral, more original, and more intellectual class of Dramatic Literature.

Having thus, perhaps somewhat at length, expressed my humble opinion, let me still further acknowledge the admiration I have felt for your private worth, reflecting as it does with infinite credit upon the profession of which you are so distinguished a member; and I entertain a sincere desire that, however humble their position, to many you may prove an example, who, in imitating your perseverance and strictly honourable conduct, must surely find an acknowledgment in the respect of their fellow creatures—thus (when comparing it with other professions) the untruthful *cant* of the "poor actor" would no more be heard, for capacity, respectability, and industry need never seek long for that encouragement responsible managers are ever willing to bestow.

These remarks, believe me, are not penned in any sycophantic spirit, but as the result of one deply interested in the subject; and who, wishing you and Mrs. Kean many years of future happiness, has the pleasure of subscribing himself,

Yours faithfully and obediently,

THE AUTHOR.

PREFACE.

During a period of some twelve or thirteen years my professional duties have rendered it necessary for me to travel over a considerable portion of Great Britain; and although my services professionally have been almost entirely confined to its larger towns, my wandering disposition has led me to employ every available day, week or month in seeking out fresh beauties or objects of interest in landscape or city, both here and on the continent. During these peregrinations it has been my lot to encounter many strange incidents, bearing with melancholy or singular interest upon the events that are ever surrounding us and our fellow-labourers—

> "In the world's broad field of battle,
> In the bivouac of life."

Month after month new faces have been near me, new acquaintances have been formed, a few weeks, or perhaps days only, have passed over, and from the inevitable force of circumstances our paths have diverged, a "farewell" has been spoken, and with few exceptions the probability has been we should never meet again. This experience is not confined to individuals of any particular sphere in life, having shared the hospitality, and I hope good-will, of almost all classes. To some few who have known me, several of the following sketches will be familiar, in the events to which they refer, and will prove, though long silent, the recollections of our companionship are not forgotten. From the reflections and circumstances of so varied a life, these and other Tales first sprung to amuse a rather large circle of friends. At their desire, I have selected and publish a few in the present form, to seek for broader sympathy. Friends are prone to be too partial — the sentence, gentle reader, now lies with you.

I certainly regret that the majority bear so sad a moral; if I could honestly have happily married my heroes and heroines, and surrounded them with thankful, chubby children, after the manner of novelists in general, I would gladly have done so; but, alas! the reality would then be wanting: truth having been my guide, I have no power to control "the divinity that shapes our ends."

Sheffield,
December, 1862.

CONTENTS.

THE SMUGGLER'S STORY.

What is the worst of woes that wait on age?
  What stamps the wrinkle deeper on the brow?
To view each lov'd one blotted from life's page,
  And be alone on earth, as I am now.

BYRON.

Long thus he chewed the cud of inward grief,
  And did consume his gall with anguish sore;
Still when he mused on his late mischief,
  Then still the smart thereof increased more,
  And seemed more grievous than it was before.

SPENSER.

"FINE weather, sir!" said a rough voice at my side, a few minutes after being comfortably seated on a stage coach, within a dozen miles of Milford Haven. "Very," I replied, turning to look at the person addressing me. He was an old man, with a face bronzed by exposure to the weather—a frank, manly, yet sad expression in it, and hair that is generally termed "iron gray." His dress was half landsman, half seaman, and in its peculiar adjustment bore unmistakeable signs of his predilections. The hat was thrown far back on his head, as if it had no right to a place there, the shirt collar turned down, exposing a brawny neck, and his neck-tie was in a sailor's knot. Indeed, at first sight he struck me as an old Jack-tar, who, having seen much service, had, against his will, been transformed into a respectable "land-lubber;" and having doffed his sou'wester and pea jacket had taken to a Moses' four-and-nine and an outrageously long-tailed coat. On recalling his features, I cannot tell what strange inducement I had for encouraging conversation, generally whilst travelling being exceedingly taciturn; but the desire at the time seemed almost irresistible—I suppose it was the appearance of the man, and his evident familiarity with "hair-breadth 'scapes," and all the dangers of a nautical life. At first he withdrew from my delicately-hinted queries; but a little tact does much, in such cases, a little brandy more, and the latter I supplied him with from a small pocket flask I carried with me. So much inducement he could not withstand, and at length we became excellent friends, an acquaintance resulting in the following story:*—

"You see yonder mountain, sir. Not that—the

* I may here remark, though to a certain extent a lover of the marvellous and romantic, I have a great horror of being made the dupe of a fable. Remembering the chief points of this story, on my visit to the town some weeks after, where the old man was residing, situated but a few miles from the scene of his adventures, I made the necessary inquiries, and am able to record them as facts.

other, more to the west, now rather obscure from the distance, There's not a foot for miles round that I am not well acquainted with. I trod it when a child, I played about it when a boy, and I lived near it as a man. My father's life was almost passed within sight of it, and to both of us it has been the wished-for landmark in many a storm, and in many a secret and dangerous enterprise. He was what you call a smuggler, sir! I don't like the name. I never did, though I, too, followed the calling, and till late years knew no other. I would as soon be called a robber at once—mayhap you think there ain't much difference—but on this point, you see, we don't all go upon the same tack. I and my father, in the whole of our lives, never defrauded the king, who is now dead and gone, God bless him! one half as much as many of these men I read about with fine names, snug berths, and enormous pay for doing nothing. They're none of 'em particular about taking more than their due when they get the chance, I take it. Well, then, the government robs the public to pay them; and it's my opinion there's many a greater rogue in the parliament house than ever I was or my father before me. But John Bull only winks at these misdeeds. At poor devils like us, he only winks when he's got us in gaol or treading the footsteps of the gallows.

"A little to the right of that mountain, some twenty years ago, standing just upon its slope, in a sort of ravine, and within some three hundred yards of the sea, was a low thatched cottage. It was a goodly size. Over its door stood a bit of a porch, and on its walls I trained roses and honeysuckles. Fore and aft there was a little flower garden, and to that garden, when not otherwise employed, I devoted the main part of my time. As long as I can remember I had a liking for flowers, and when a boy could tell many of their names as they ought to be called. It may seem a bit of contradiction in nature—that a man who followed a lawless calling like a smuggler's, who daily and nightly braved danger, until it became almost a part of his life, should care for and tend to such little bits of things as flowers; but let it convince you, sir, that such men sometimes have hearts as well as other people.

"In that cottage my father lived and died. He had been well to do, and saved a bit of money, enough, had it been mine, to have bought a trim little vessel to trade along the coast with, as when a boy I often thought of doing; but it was not to be, sir. A rascally lawyer palavered him out of it with false pretences. He persuaded him it warn't safe in his hands; he'd invest it in some outlandish scheme and make more of it. So dad thought he was doing a good thing, and gave it to the lawyer's care. He not only got rid of it, because he said the speculation failed, but he made dad pay for doing so, which he couldn't understand no how. When the old man died I had a young wife and child to keep, and only the old cottage to commence my first cruise with. I had always a tough will and a ready hand. I became a smuggler on my own account, and before a year had passed I owned as trim a little craft as ever spread her canvas to the breeze or gave the revenue sharks the slip. I have been in her when the sea rolled mountains high, as the saying goes, when the best ship in His Majesty's service would have scarcely weathered the storm, and have felt myself as safe as if I had been floating on a duck pond; and many a time, when chased by a royal cutter, the saucy little clipper stood on her way, scarcely veering a point till she snugly laid up in some secure and secret port, known only to her helmsman and her crew.

"In those days I was known about these parts as Dare-devil Will. Three different times they made me acquainted with the county gaol, but I soon found my way out. And how do you think I did it, sir? Why, the magistrates about this quarter knew it was more than they dare do to commit me. Several of them and many of the gentry about here were in the habit, and had been for years, of buying a sly keg or two. To oblige them in this way I often ran great risks; and as one good turn deserves another, I took care to jog their memory when their help was needed. One of these magistrates was a parson, as jolly an old rogue as ever lived, who hated three-quarter grog as he hated old Nick, and had a monstrous liking for the real nateral spirit and prime bacca. Many's the run he's had his share of.

" There's an old saying, ' set a thief to catch a thief.' So say I, " set a rogue to beat a rogue," if you want him well flogged. Thus it was with the parson; he was known to be the most severe magistrate for many miles round, and would send a poor devil to gaol, without mercy, guilty or innocent; if he was suffering from indigestion; or if he happened to be kept waiting five minutes beyond his dinner hour, it was certain to add another six weeks to his victim; and if he once got his grappling irons athwart you, you might as well pray to a stone wall. It so happened that one of the revenue men, Tom Jones, had a sort of half-witted nephew; the poor lad was fatherless and motherless, and must have starved, but for the kindness of his uncle; and the neighbours for miles round, they all knew him, and gave him the kind word and sup. He was a crazy, wild mountain sort of colt. I have met him many a dark and stormy night, wandering barefoot about the hills, the rocks, and the sea shore, his clothes hanging in rags about him, as they had been torn by his scrambling through the briars, or clambering the highest cliffs; he looked so weird-like then, with his long hair streaming behind him, he has startled me, standing a solitary object on some high rock, shouting with glee as the lightning shot about him. I sometimes thought the very devil himself was in the poor boy's soul. You must not think he was neglected, sir; far from it: at his uncle's he had a comfortable home, but he never cared to stay there, he was only happy when wandering. Well, it so happened, one night, the parson lost two or three fowls, and this poor lad was the last person seen near his house; he was accordingly taken up and tried for robbery. We all strove to get him off, and the parson knew he was a silly creature; but it was no use, he happened to be a little bilious that morning, with drinking too much smuggled rum, I suppose, over night, and he sent him to prison for a long time. God only knows what he suffered there! He had neither the sense nor the chance to tell; but I leave you to judge something of what his wild nature felt, when he saw the bright moon shining between his prison bars, for, one morning, like a caged bird, against the walls he had beaten himself to death. It was a cruel act, sir, of the parson : I always thought so, and when I had the chance, afterwards, I didn't forget to give him a lift for it.

"Tom Jones took on sadly about the matter, and it being somehow suspected that the parson, did a little business with me, on the sly, he resolved to watch for his opportunity and have his revenge. A couple of months after this event, I had a first-rate run of the right sort of stuff, and the old chap wanted a keg or two, besides some bacca. I knew Tom was on the look out, and had sworn he wouldn't let a chance slip, so what to do, I was a bit run-a-ground. At last, I hit upon the plan of dressing up my son Ben as a woman, who was then a strapping, good-looking lad of sixteen. We got a cart, and doing so, put him in it—my old woman first having given him a lesson in nursing. The bacca we put in a bag and clapped it on Ben's starn, a six-gallon keg we put in a feather bed, having first taken out some of its innards, and on this the boy was to lay, the big part, where the keg was, for a pillow. A small keg we rigged out for a child: this, Ben was to dandle. When all was ship-shape, away we started; it was getting dark, and just as I was entering the old parson's plantation, out rushes Tom Jones, with a couple of mates at his elbow, and seizes hold of the horse's head.

"'Hilloa!' said Tom, 'so Master Will, I have caught you at last, have I? and the old thief up there is one of your crew, is he?—curse me, if I didn't think so!'

"'Why, Tom,' said I, 'you are not altogether right in your figure head, I take it—what are you coming athwart me in this shape for?'

"'None of your palaver,' replied Tom, 'I'm not a younker; you are not going to come over me, I can tell yer; you have done it before, I know, but you don't do it again, so mates, look to the cart, there.'

"At this moment, Ben let out a groan or two, in the bottom of it.

"'By the powers!' said an Irishman, one of Tom's mates, 'if he hasn't got a dead body there, I hear it a-groanin—here's been murther, anyhow.'

"'So there's been throat-cutting too, Will, has there? What will the old swab of a parson say to that? I thought you'd be hanged one day, and now I'm sure of it—let's look, mate, at the murdered body. Shew a light here, will yer!'

"'Ochone! ochone!' shouted the Irishman, holding up the lantern, 'sure, its a female woman, the bla'guards have kilt a woman. Now, by my soul, I hope they'll be scragged! Tom, look, she's not kilt, for see how she's a-groanin.'

"'Oh! oh! oh!' from Ben in the cart. On going to them, I found they were about hauling him out, so drawing Tom aside, I whispered in his ear, at which he started, and ordering his shipmates to desist, came with me a little to the fore of the cart.

"'Shipmates!' said I, 'don't disturb that poor lass. I know there's no ill-feeling existing between us, except in the way of duty, and I know, too, you have got a bit of spite against the old parson, here; to tell you the truth, we are no cater cousins. I hate the old beggar, for his treatment of poor Mad Tommy; you're on the wrong scent to-night; take a pull at the bottle, whilst I let you into the secret.'

"'What!' blazed out Tom, 'drink smuggled brandy? damme, what do you take me for? d'ye think I ain't got no conscience?' It was a weak one, I knew, on this point, for Tom was a rare one at his grog.

"'Niver mind your conscience, this time, there's nobody a-lookin,' exclaimed the Irishman, 'it's not convanient, on a cold night like this; I'll take a pull, Will, anyhow. Here's long life to yer, and may you niver die by a hempen noose.' After taking a long pull, he smacked his lips—"Oh, Holy St. Patrick, Tom! that's the stuff to warm the cockles of your heart!'

"Poor Tom's scruples couldn't stand it any

longer; he seized hold of the bottle, just as the Irishman was about to repeat the dose.

"'Well,' said Tom, 'its a bad example, Pat, and I only drink to keep you sober; for your sake I'll drown my conscience in the spirit, so go a-head with the yarn, Will." 'Shipmates,' I continued, 'you must know this poor lass comes one night, to my cottage, with that there piccaninny in her arms. She hangs out signals of distress, and tells my wife, as how she's been ruined by the parson, who had cruelly deserted her, after her giving birth to the younker, a real strong one he is too, I can tell yer. So, taking pity on the lass, I slung her a hammock. Well, ever since, she seemed in a queer way, so thinks I, why shouldn't the swab pay for his own villany. So, you see, we claps her into the cart, on a feather bed, with the picaninny in her arms, and now I'm taking her to give the old chap a surprise.'

"Tom Jones was overcome with joy on hearing this yarn, and vowed it should be all over the country before the morrow. This was the very thing I wanted; for I wished to serve him out for sending the poor idiot to gaol.

"'Poor lass,' said Tom, looking at Ben, in the cart, 'she's a fine lass, mate, rather big about the starn, though,'—this part of Ben being uppermost, with the bacca.

" 'Yes,' cried Pat, 'an the divil a bit will she let you see her face.'

" 'No,' I replied, 'like enough, messmates, she's shamefaced, poor thing.'

" 'No wonder,' said Tom, 'so will you be, Pat, if you ever get in her sitiation.' At which Pat shook and scratched his head, looked at Ben and the child, and seemed to wonder whether it was ever likely.

" 'Well, give us your fist,' continued Tom, 'I respect you for sarving that old swab out; but I say, don't try to come over me again, 'cos it won't answer, and though I don't wish you any harm, I know I shall nab you one of these days, so look out. You see, I'm an old tar, and ain't to be palavered no how. Here, shipmate, hold up the glim, let's take another peep into the cart, and see all's fair and square.'

" They looked at Ben again, and there he lay, nursing the picaninny with the brandy in its innards, as nat'ral as could be. So the old tar, as was'nt to be come over, says, 'Never mind, lass, never mind, the old swab as ruined you shall set you ship-shape again, or my name's not Tom Jones.' Then away he and his mates steer, as nicely come over, I flatter myself, as ever they were in their lives. When the decks were clear Ben unships his toggery, removes the bacca, and we takes it up to the parson's house, who the next morning woke to find himself notorious as the father of a chance child whose mother he had sent adrift; and for years afterwards he was rated by the men, and abused by the women. He swore it was false — and he could swear, when he had a mind, I can tell you—but no one believed him; whilst strong suspicions got afloat that he'd murdered the mother, as no one could discover who or where she was. One fine morning, too, the whole country was in arms, for it was said her bones were dug up in his cabbage garden; but it turned out to be only the remains of a leg of mutton, which had been stolen and buried there by his dog, 'Snap.'

"When my wife died, Ben was the only creature left me in the world to care for, and I loved him, sir, with all the love a father can feel for an only child. At two-and-twenty he wanted to get married, and settled like, so he anchored his hopes upon a trim little lass, a servant to some very respectable people living close at hand. She was an orphan, as honest and good a girl as ever lived; yet, somehow, I couldn't bear the idea of their getting spliced: it seemed to me, in my selfish nature, another had no right to share my boy's love. It was a sort of dog-in-the-manger wish, I dare say, that he should waste his days on such an old hulk as I was; but had you seen him, and felt as I did, you might have blamed, but you could not have wondered. He was as tall and good-looking a lad, as you would wish to see. I have never met with his like for strength, and after his mother's death he proved a kind companion and a stanch friend. Such a shipmate to bear one company in all weathers, rough or smooth, with a cheerful heart and willing hand, is not often met with. At last, Ben proposed he should bring his wife home to the cottage, and they should live there still, as my children. To this I consented. The marriage day was fixed. Poor Mary commenced operations to furbish up her scanty wardrobe, and set it shipshape for her new situation. As to Ben, he was all adrift up aloft, and could think or talk of nothing else but the haven of happiness he was steering for. Well, sir, the day came, and found us as merry as well could be. The old parson spliced them together; the girls had a good blubber about it, though what for I don't know, unless it was because they warn't in the same predicament. Poor Ben, he looked as big a fool as well could be. There was Mary, too, so clean, and pretty, that I loved and forgave her, though she had taken a link out (and that the main one) from the cable which bound father and son together. As for myself, I was rigged out in new clothes; that was the most uncomfortable part of the affair, for I felt much like a pig in armour; however, I didn't mind being bottled up for an hour or two, my lad seemed so happy.

"When the neighbours drank to him and his bride, 'A long life and a merry one,' he looked at her so hopeful, like, as if he saw that life as clear afore him as if his hand was at the helm, and the shoals and quicksands over which he must pass were dangers unthought of, uncared for. Ah! at that moment, could I have owned the trimmest fleet that ever sailed out of the Downs to fight the enemies of England. I could not have been prouder and happier, and I wouldn't have made the exchange. You are, of course, a stranger to such feelings they are sad ones now, and the leaf in the log book of my memory where these few hours are written—the happiest I ever spent—will be the last one I shall turn over when I am piped to my duty in the other world."

The old man here paused, and I could see the tears flowing down his weather-beaten cheeks. Deeming such sorrow sacred, I waited in silence till he resumed :—

"About the time of Ben's marriage, we were expecting a cargo over from France; and sure enough, that very night, when we were all dancing as merry as crickets, one of my mates, who had been on the look-out, rushed in with the news that he could just discern the cutter in the offing. So I doffed my fine clothes, and was just making all sail with Ben—the rest of the guests, being mostly comrades, had gone home to do the same—when Mary came and flung her arms round his neck, and looking up into his face, like a frightened child, said: 'Ben, dear, don't go! for my sake, for your own, dear Ben, pray, don't! Indeed, indeed, something dreadful will happen!' I thought it only the silly ravings of a girl, and felt half angry that Ben, who had been used to danger since his childhood, should listen to her, or that his cheeks should go pale, which I could see they did, by the light of the lantern hanging over his head; but the next moment I was sorry for having doubted his courage, for, like the true-hearted lad he ever was, he gently put her aside, and replied: 'Mary, don't be frightened, lass; father is going, and if he is not afraid, why should I be? There, calm thee girl, I shall soon be back; and with a few more lucky runs, there'll be an end of this sort of life.' The boy had spoken truly: I had determined, for his sake, to leave off smuggling—for it was dangerous work at best—and trade along the coast. 'That end may be nearer than thee thinks,' said Mary. 'Indeed, indeed, for God's sake, listen to me and do not go.' Ay, how she did cling to him! As I looked in her face that moment there seemed something so strange—so warning, like, it made me shudder—turn cold even to my heart. I can feel that coldness sometimes now, when I'm alone and thinking, as I often do, over that fearful night. When I was a boy I remembered seeing an old woman, who they said was a witch; she used to tell folks when they were going to die. She told my grandfather because he refused to cross her hand with a piece of silver; and I was with him when she did so. Sure enough, about the time she said, he died. I didn't believe in her witchery for all that. Yet, though Mary's face was fair, young, and plump, and the old hag's yellow, thin, and haggard in the look, I seemed to see the same foretelling power. Though years had separated the events, though I had scarcely thought of the old hag since, it flashed athwart my mind, together with the truth of the old crone's prophecy.

"'Ben,' said I, 'never mind me, lad, it's your marriage night, and Mary, poor lass, is scared. We'll land the stuff safe without you; no harm will come to me.' At this moment, crash! came the door, as it was blown open by a sudden gust of wind. I started up, and Mary clung more closely to Ben. It was some few moments before I recovered myself enough to speak. There seemed summat very strange about it. When I did so, I walked to the door and looked out into the darkness. Not a sound could I hear but the wind whistling through a few old trees which grew thereabouts. It had shifted since evening, and was blowing a bit of a gale. The sea was rolling on the beach or lashing the rocks, and the rain fell pattering on the roof and the little porch of my cottage, or dripped from leaf to leaf on the high rosetrees of my garden. It looked black enough, but it had looked as dismal many a time before, and never cost me a thought. All at once, a long low whistle came from the direction of the sea. It was the signal. The cutter was creeping in along shore, and not a moment was to be lost.

"'There's the signal, Ben ; will you stay with Mary or go with me?' I asked. 'My lass, replied the boy, as he released her arms, 'don't make me a coward for the first time in my life.' What will my comrades say? Father, I'm with you. God bless the girl! We shall be soon back.' We started through the rain and darkness. Just at the slope of the hill, before losing sight of the cottage, I looked in Ben's face, as the moon was just peeping from behind a cloud. It was much paler than I had ever seen it, and he was looking behind him at Mary, who was still standing at the doorway, her figure looking clear and distinct against the fire and lamplight of the room. A second signal then came, and away we ran to join our messmates.

"The part of the beach where they were waiting was perhaps the most lonely spot along this line of coast. The water, though generally deep, required an old and sure hand to steer clear of the rocks; when once in though, it would take a sharp look-out to discover a craft at anchor. Heaven only knows how many a fine cargo my dad and myself had helped in there. On one side rose a high cliff. At its foot, facing the sea, was a tolerably deep cavern, used by us for signals and for stowing away lumber. On the other side was a steep slope, covered with trees, and facing inland was another thick with brushwood, and a dried-up mill-stream in its centre, with high moss and gorse-covered banks. On our meeting our mates, we could see the cutter slowly making her way within a few yards of the shore. Scarcely a minute had elapsed before her anchor was let go, a hawser cast on land, and all was ready to unship her cargo. To it we went, keg after keg came ashore; not a voice broke through the silence, for we were too intent on the work. Not a torch was used, with the exception of one kept burning in the cave. The rain had changed to a drizzling sort of shower —the wind came moaning along the dry mill-stream

—the last keg of a goodly lot was being hauled in by Ben, when of a sudden a low whistle was heard—it made us all start. I did not like the sound, and listened till I could hear my heart beat against my ribs. It was not cowardice—for I defy any man to accuse me of that—but it brought with it, all at once, Mary and her warning, and the old witch's prophecy. A few minutes and a second whistle came from a distance. Too well I guessed its meaning—the revenue sharks were upon us. In a moment the cutter was set adrift and stood out to sea. My mates and myself knew if we were taken it would be all Davy Jones with us, so we resolved to have a tussle for it. At that moment a sudden flash came from amongst the trees to our left. The aim was a sure one, for, with a deep groan, a comrade fell by my side. The next minute we were fighting hand to hand. My shipmates knew one of their number lay in his blood, and they fought not only for liberty but revenge. In the darkness friends were hardly discernible from foes, and many a blow was given and received by messmates. It must have been a strange wild scene, sir—men fighting like tigers on a desolate sea shore, with the rain falling and the wind howling. In half the time I have taken to tell it all was over, and I found myself a prisoner in the arms of two powerful sailors. My first thought was for Ben. I called his name, but my voice seemed to die up the old mill-stream in an echo—again I called, but Ben was silent. With the strength of a lion I broke from the grapnels that held me, and fled up the bank. For some little distance I could hear the king's men at my heels, but putting them on the wrong tack I steered for the cottage, and rushing in found Mary, poor lass, with her face so white and scared, crying and moaning over the half-burnt logs upon the hearth. She started up with a scream on catching sight of my figure-head, and flinging her arms around my neck, shrieked out, 'Father, dear father, tell me what has happened?'

"'Nothing, lass, nothing,' I replied, with a choking voice, as I looked about anxiously to see if my boy was there.

"'You have killed him! you have killed him!' she cried, 'I see it all now. God help me! God help me!' and starting from me, as if I had really murdered him—I who loved him so much—she fell on her knees, hiding her face in her hands, and weeping as though her poor little heart would break, whilst my throat grew parched, and my eyes went dim, not with tears—no, no—not with tears, for they would have brought relief, but with anguish too deep for tears; and murmuring, 'I will go and seek him,' I fled once more into the open air.

The breeze cooled my burning brain, and I rushed down towards the beach. It was all quiet now. Not a living thing remained upon the spot, where only a few minutes before I and others had been fighting like tigers. My shipmates had mostly been taken prisoners; some had escaped. Could Ben have done so? No, for he would at once have steered for the cottage. As I stood thus thinking, hardly knowing what to do, or where to turn for help, I saw a dark thing lying upon the yellow sand. It seemed motionless. I looked again; it was the outline of a man, and I thought of my poor boy. I ran and got the torch that still burned in the cave. I felt blind with fear. It was not Ben, but one of the revenue men, who, poor fellow, had died in doing his duty. I pitied him, and hoped it was not my own hand that struck him down, for blood is a terrible thing to have on the conscience. One of our men had been struck with a bullet at my side, I remembered. Who could that have been? I did not search long for the truth. Another dark form lay not far off, and holding up the torch I could see the colour of the clothes and recognise them. I went to the body, turned it over on its face, and looked upon my son, he who had been my companion through so many years, the bridegroom of a few hours! The eyes that I had seen so full of love and happiness now fixed in death. They seemed to look on me with reproach; I thought, even, they accused me of the murder. The red glare of the torch fell upon his face—so white, sir, so very white! I shall never forget it. Even now sometimes at night, or in my dreams, the look comes back to me. I felt I had led a bad life: this was my punishment: and sinking on my knees, perhaps for the first time in my life, I prayed that God would forgive me."

The old man paused to wipe the perspiration from his brow, where it had settled thick as dew; and after a pause he proceeded:—

"Taking up the body I lifted it on my shoulder, and took my way up the old mill-stream towards the cottage. The rain had ceased, and the rays of the moon fell upon me and my dreadful burthen. I had not proceeded far before a something warm slowly trickling down my face made me stop. I thought at first it was perspiration, and drew my hand across to remove it. The hand was red with blood—the blood of my boy. From side to side I shifted the body to escape the stream, but still I felt it, creeping, so slowly; though but a few drops, to me it seemed a river. At length I reached the cottage, where but a few hours back we were so happy—where friends had met to wish him joy, and years of future bliss. Where was the joy, the hope, the bliss now? All gone! Foundered on a rock—lost on the ocean of eternity!

"To the bride of a few hours I took him, placed him quietly on his bed, where poor Mary, moaning and sobbing, threw herself at his side, laid his head upon her breast, lulling him, like a child, to sleep. Poor girl! as yet she only dreamt—the scene was too terrible for her to believe. In my own heart I almost wished she might never wake again to feel her loss. As for myself, I had but one wish—to be struck down dead beside him. So hours went past, till a loud knocking came to the door. Too well I knew its meaning, and running to the door, I placed a small beam of wood athwart it, and barred the shutters. I thought to defend my home whilst a stone remained; but they would not be beaten—they fired the cottage, and I saw the flames creeping slowly, then quickly over windows, door, and roof; I saw the ground about red with the threatening flame, and then I thought of the living and the dead, so near and dear to me. For myself I cared not, but the poor lass, her fate was sad enough already, and heaven forbid that I should look upon her perishing in the flames, so I took down the beam from the door—the king's men rushed in, and dragged me away to gaol. My story, now, is soon ended. I told you the way I slipped through the hands of the magistrates before; I did so again, although it was a hard matter this time, for you see, blood had been spilt. I was in prison for months, and the guineas had to flow pretty freely from the pockets of my patrons, before what you call justice thought herself sufficiently bribed to let me slip through her fingers. Once free, with an anxious heart my first steps were towards my cottage, and it stood before me, a blackened hull—a wreck, deserted and desolate, its ruined walls covering the ashes of my boy; and one rose-tree still bloomed in the little garden, the lone and only living monument of all the days and years, the joys and sorrows, which had been passed and felt beneath that humble roof.

In the village I heard Mary had been taken, kept for some time, and then sent to a distant part of the country, by the kind folks she had before lived with. I have never seen or heard from her since. As to myself, I took to an honest calling—friends started up, where they were least expected, and fortune has smiled upon me when I seemed to have little need of it; but I mustn't complain, there is one, and the only harbour, left, which I hope to reach at last, with a fair wind and clean heart. I am now steering for it—quickly, sir—quickly."

"What harbour, is that?" I asked.

His answer was—"The grave!"

THE LOST DEED.

He that of greatest works is Finisher
Oft does them by the weakest minister!
So Holy Writ in babes hath judgment shown,
When judges have been babes. Great floods have flown
From simple sources; and great seas have dried,
When miracles have by the greatest been denied.
Oft expectation fails, and most oft there
Where most it promises; and oft it hits,
Where hope is coldest, and despair most sits.

SHAKESPEARE.

How often events, by chance and unexpectedly, come to pass,
Which you had not dared even to hope for!

TERENCE.

MANY years ago, there lived in the village of W——, in one of the midland counties, a Squire Wilton; as jovial an old representative of that now extinct race, as ever made the hills and valleys echo with the huntsman's cheer. I say extinct, because we have no thorough-bred fox-hunting squires now-a-days. I believe they went out with breeches and top boots. The whole aspect of country life is changed. Now, no well-to-do farmer but gives his son a college, or at least a boarding-school, education. In the days of which I speak, such things were little thought of; as long as Tom, or Dick,

Harry, or Bob could ride, smoke, shoot, drink, swear, hunt, and knew something of farming, write his own name, and spell a word of two syllables, his education was complete. We certainly had no railways, then; and the facility for intercourse with large towns has done much to refine the habits of our forefathers. It has taken away much that was evil, and, alas, too! introduced many fashionable follies, that were never thought of by our more primitive relations. In a puff of smoke we are now wafted up to London; then we had bad roads and rickety stage coaches, or brilliant four-horse stages, with their red-coated, horn-blowing, perquisite-receiving guards and drivers. A journey to London was a case of deep reflection and will-making; now, it is an "I-shall-be-back-to-night" affair. However, to continue my story: Squire Wilton was one of the old school, and though he had lost his wife, and an only son, (a very fine young fellow, the old gossips say---who broke his neck taking a stream), still laughed, still drank, and still swore, and was only kept in order by a wizen-faced old lady, the housekeeping fixture of the establishment, whom he regarded as the necessary evil of his life, and to whom he submitted as to no other mortal. She was often known to send him blustering to bed, in the middle of some drunken bout, amidst the ridicule and uproarious laughter of his companions, who generally had to finish their mirth on the outside of the door, whence they were summarily ejected by the indignant shrew.

Little as such an idea may coincide with these proceedings, old Squire Wilton and Dame Margery were adored by the poor, for miles round, few ever asking a favour in vain, or leaving the old hall with an empty stomach. He was, besides, a liberal master, and by this means bound his labourers to his service, heart and soul.

One of the sweetest spots, in or near the village, were the almshouses. They were the gift of an old maid, and consisted of seven habitations, built in the old English gable-thatched style, with casement windows, and quaint-looking chimneys—whilst over the walls of each, twined the rose, honeysuckle, or ivy. They stood detached, surrounding a smooth, green, circular lawn, and each boasting a trim little flower garden of its own. What a good, kind old maid this must have been! I have often said, Bless her! as I looked at her gift, and the poor old people she had benefited. Near to the almshouses was a large field, consisting of several acres, which belonged to Squire Wilton; and some few years previous to his death, an officious Magog of the village impounded a poor man's donkey for grazing there. This functionary, in reporting the same to the squire, instead of receiving an acknowledgment in thanks, or lucre, for his zeal, was threatened with a kick on the breech if he meddled with that animal again, or any other. And the squire, finding from the owner that the detention of the donkey had caused considerable loss to him, at once sent for his lawyer to draw up a deed of gift, bestowing the field entire, as a freehold, for the sole use and benefit of the poor folks of the village. The deed was then deposited in the hands of Lawyer Quirk, for his safe keeping, who was supposed to place the same in one of the musty, rusty, iron-bound boxes, containing the acts and deeds, the hopes and fears, of the surrounding squirearchy, and their successors. Now must we wave the enchanter's wand, and 'ere the sand could turn within its hour glass, add twenty years to our story. The old squire had claimed his last inheritance: as Shakespeare says—

> "Nothing can we call our own, but death,
> And that small model of the barren earth
> Which serves as paste and cover to our bones."

He had found that cover in the tomb of his ancestors. The old housekeeper, too, had passed away, and in the church-yard might be seen the stone covering her grave, and on it an epitaph desiring the passer-by to stay and shed a tear—not a very likely thing for any one to do. Indeed, it has always seemed to me a very foolish, though very common request in such places. Phineas Quirk, the lawyer, he too had been dead ten or a dozen years. The house in which he had imparted to the rich, "the expensive luxury" of his profession, had been turned "inside out," to quote a rather impossible phrase, and was now a village beershop. The old red-brick dirty genteel building had lost the last remains of its respectability, and stood a ruinous monument of the many anxious hearts that had once crossed its threshold. The successor to his practice was a dapper, shrewd little gentleman, of the name of Crawsuit. He inhabited a dapper little house, a sort of cross between the high and low gentry's residences. On his door he boasted a large brass plate, cleaned every morning until you could see your face in it; and as members of his household, he had a wife and maid-servant. Like Lawyer Quirk, Squire Wilton had found a successor in a distant relation, once a great *roue*, when he had nothing of his own to spend, but who, on becoming a great landholder, was transmogrified into a religious rogue, a man without a particle of true Christian principle in his composition, who, like many others, clothed his parsimony, his oppression, and his hypocrisy in black cloth, and smothered each generous feeling in the ample starched folds of his white neckcloth ; a being who, if he had been measured by the principle of Lavater, that "the more honesty a man has the less he affects the air of a saint," (a principle I highly esteem) would have been found entirely wanting.

The first act of this sanctimonious petrefaction was to urge a continued war against the poor, who claimed and enjoyed the right of use of the field bestowed upon them by the squire. Unfortunately it was not long before he discovered the deed of gift was wanting. It had not been found amongst the late Lawyer Quirk's papers, nor seen since his death. Upon this discovery he asserted his claim. The parish failed to maintain its right, and so the poor, much to their discomfiture, lost the land.

Having thus laid the foundation of my story, I resume it nine years after the said trial, and twenty-nine years after the first grant of the disputed property. It so happened in this village, as in most others, a great rivalry existed between the houses of Crawsuit, the lawyer, and Pimple, the doctor, both factions being headed, as a matter of course, by the respective wives : whatever one did, the other deemed it the business of her life, for the time being, to outdo. By this means a continuous civil war was carried on under the most seeming friendly colours. If Mrs. Pimple owned a peculiar china teapot, Mrs. Crawsuit must have a still more peculiar china teapot. If Mrs. Pimple claimed her descent in a direct line from somebody who landed with William the Conqueror, Mrs. Crawsuit could prove hers with somebody who came over with the Romans. If one had disease of the head, the other had disease of the heart. One thing certainly Mrs. Pimple had a right to feel proud of—she had two children—two fine children. Mrs. Crawsuit was childless. She had only dreamt of having one once, and then it was a mistake. Keenly did Mrs. C. feel this, and much occasionally did she reproach her husband with the fact, who, poor man, always replied with a bland smile, "He couldn't help it." All this, though very exciting to the two ladies, was the cause of unceasing annoyance to their husbands, who would like to have been on really friendly and neighbourly terms.

Under these circumstances, judge of the height to which Mrs. Crawsuit's combative genius rose on discovering, one fine morning, a lilliputian greenhouse in the course of erection by the side of Pimple's house. Her husband was dragged out of bed to look at it, and was sent into bed again with a torrent of indignation, because he simply replied, "he dare say it would look very nice!" Then, this wise individual, feeling he had offended, turned over against the wall, went to sleep again, dreamt of "Roe versus Doe," forgot all about the greenhouse and Mrs. Crawsuit too.

Mrs. C. in the mean time formed her own plans. A friendly visit was paid that morning to inquire after the health of Johnny Pimple, who had got the measles. Mrs. C. remained calm even under the stinging sarcasm, "and how is your— Dear me, how stupid I am, MY DEAR!—I was going to say, child. I was really forgetting. You have no little darlings." She coloured, bit her lip, and hugged, with apparent warmth, little Florence Pimple; but that was all. The conversation, of course, naturally turned upon the greenhouse. It was a merely casual remark, apparently; but Mrs. P. "really had nothing to do with it"—in reply—"it was her husband's doing." Mrs. C. knew better, and stood to her guns; but, after a series of unsuccessful circumlocutive attacks and cunning repulses, she retired in high dudgeon, to vent her ill temper on the receiver-general—her husband being out of the way—her maid of all work! One determination had certainly been arrived at, "she'd have a greenhouse or know the reason why. If Mr. Crawsuit did not consent not a moment's peace should he have." The dapper little lawyer, quite innocent of the intended outrage upon his domestic felicity, finished a hard day's work, and sat himself down in his easy chair to have his tea and read the *Times*, his constant habit, when the enemy drew near and opened fire.

"Well, James, dear," began the lady, "I've been over to see Mrs. Pimple's greenhouse." "Have you, my love?" replied the husband, in a tone somewhat removed from pleasure at the announcement, experience having taught him what to expect. "Yes, I have, indeed!" continued Mrs. C., "and I really never saw such airs in my life as the Pimples give themselves; for all the world as if others could not have a greenhouse as well."

"Humph!" he ejaculated, scratching his head, and diving deeper into the paper.

"I really have not common patience with such stuck-up people, have you, dear?"

Thus directly appealed to, he was obliged to reply, and a noise between a grunt and a growl issued from behind the mighty sheets of the "*Times*."

"I did not ask you to grunt, dear, but to speak," said Mrs. Crawsuit, in a warning tone.

"Grunt, my dear! you are mistaken in using such an expression; but, really, don't say any more about it this evening; I've a most interesting and important case to read—Tomkins *versus* Gingerapple — and it is absolutely necessary I should render myself intimately acquainted with its details; it involves——'

"It involves fiddlesticks!" interrupted his spouse. "It is always the way I am treated when I sit down to have an agreeable chat. I might as well not be married at all, as have a husband who is read, read, read, from morning until night, neglecting his poor wife. No one else would be such a fool as I have been, to stand it. You know how meek-tempered I am, and that is the reason you impose upon me. I was happy enough before I married you."

"Well, well," replied Crawsuit, soothingly, "I am so used to these *agreeable* chats, you see, unfortunately, they generally end the same way—my pockets; and I am not rich."

"Not rich, indeed! You can waste your money in other ways; but let your poor wife ask for a trifle, and you never can afford it. I have been a good wife to you: when I am gone——

"Oh, bother!" exclaimed Crawsuit, "don't make a fool of yourself." These last words were accompanied with a look indignant husbands sometimes venture to assume, as much as to say—"Now, madam, I flatter myself, you can't answer that!" This is a mistake husbands often make. What will wives not answer, in order to have the last word? Without hesitation, on the present occasion the little man had a Roland for his Oliver.

"It is no matter, James, what I make of MYself: I might have had children; what would you have done then, I should like to know? I left a good home, to sacrifice myself to you, and one day you will know my value; but never mind, never mind; it was only yesterday I looked all over your shirts, and sewed on the buttons;—never mind, you'll break my heart, and then be satisfied!" Here she burst into an hysterical fit of weeping. This is, in most instances, an excellent panacea adopted on such occasions; few men like to see a woman crying, and the dapper little lawyer had a great horror of it; he had positively been known to stop badgering a witness under similar circumstances. Of course Mrs. Crawsuit knew the weakness, and lost no opportunity of profiting by the same.

"Now, for heaven's sake be quiet, there's a dear," said he with the air of a martyr, "don't cry; you know how it annoys me."

"How should I know it?" asked Mrs. Crawsuit, "your conduct, Mr. Crawsuit, teaches me otherwise."

"Well, you know I don't mean anything; how silly you are!"

"Then I may have a greenhouse, dear?" exclaimed Mrs. C., stifling her sobs and drying up her tears, at the same time going to C. and smoothing down his hair. If you, reader, should happen to be a married man, I dare say you know the knack ladies have of doing this sort of thing when they want to wheedle something out of you, and its extraordinary and irrisistible influence; then comes the musically persuasive voice, to hear it—to feel the soft hand—Oh, the artfulness of the sex! What have you done? Why, I take it, much the same as Lawyer Crawsuit did, when he said, "Yes, my dear, you may; but don't bother me any more."

The night following this conversation proved a most anxious one to the lady,—in what could she excel the Pimples? "Should she have a handsome chimney-pot stuck on her greenhouse?" but then there was no chimney; that would be no use. "Should she have a weathercock?" that was hardly the thing. At any rate, early the following morning that very useful species of the biped tribe, denominated maid-of-all-work, and christened Susan, was despatched for John Jones, the legitimate carpenter of the village. Now, Robert Short was the one employed by the Pimple family, who, being a recent importation, and intruder, was regarded as an impertinent humbug by the said John Jones. Great had been the latter's indignation on beholding the gradual development of the greenhouse, which he had inspected every morning, at five o'clock, before the other came to work. Equally great was the sudden revulsion of feeling experienced by him, on finding he had the like opportunity of displaying his skill; and in order to evince his workmanlike superiority, he, much to the gratification of his employer, lost no time or exertion to succeed. Such was the position of affairs when John Jones, on one particular occasion, retired from labour, at twelve o'clock, to refresh the inner man—that being his dinner hour. He had hardly turned his back, before Mrs. Crawsuit took advantage of his absence, (there being no convenient room for two in the greenhouse at the same time), to survey the edifice, and in her mind's eye, compare its points to that of the Pimples'. Whilst standing inside, thus engaged, her eye suddenly rested on the dirty bit of paper, or parchment, forming John Jones's working cap, which he had removed from his head, and left on a half-finished flower stand. Now a dirty workman's cap is by no means an attractive or agreeable object for a lady to scan minutely, yet Mrs. Crawsuit was an inquisitive woman—a woman who began life in the belief, "It's never too late to learn, and no opportunity should be despised." It must have been a much stronger obstacle than the present to keep her inquiring mind from examining that old cap. She lifted it daintily with finger and thumb, and her quick experienced eye at once detected the hand-writing to be a lawyer's, though the ink had faded, and was begrimed almost to illegibility. There were some names, too, attracted her attention: they were those of Squire Wilton and Lawyer Quirk; but the folds hid much more.

"Dear me!" soliloquized Mrs. Crawsuit, "what can this be, I should like to know. Drat the folds! I wonder whether I could undo them and remake it again. It is parchment. Perhaps it is a—a—really, I don't know what; but there is no harm in seeing." No sooner said than done. She read a few words; a few words more; and then, Columbus himself, on discovering the new world, could not have been more delighted. Away at once she flew to her husband, who happened to be at home. The husband at first thought her out of her senses, but on carefully examining the cap, admitted otherwise. A conference was held. The dapper lawyer, with the air of a king, enthroned himself in the large arm-chair of the back parlour, dignified into "the study," to await some great and most important event. John Jones at length returned from dinner, and was taken in custody immediately by Mrs. Crawsuit and the maid: his ejaculations of astonishment or notes of inquiry were unheeded. Susan had positively secured the broom in case of any resistance, and thus he was led captive into the presence of the lawyer.

"That will do, my dear, that will do," slowly and grandiloquently spoke Crawsuit, addressing his wife; for however he gave way when in the domestic sphere, in his professional capacity he never forgot his dignity, so he pointed to the door, intimating her absence was desirable.

"But, James, my dear, as the discoverer, my place is—

"Outside the door, my love; women know nothing of business." Much against the lady's inclination he conducted her to the passage, re-entered the room, and closed the door. John Jones looked on meanwhile in the utmost amazement, inwardly recalling the past to discover a clue. Visions of suspected murder or midnight robbery filled his imagination, and though a big fellow, he trembled at the glance the lawyer threw at him. Like a man dreaming, the circumstances of a lifetime rushed into his brain; but he could find no explanation of the present mystery.

"Your name is John Jones?" said Mr. C., having resumed his seat.

"Yes, sir; and I hope"—

"Silence, sir, and answer my questions, if you please."

" But I thought"—

" You have no right to think. You are a native of this village ?"

" Ye—e—s, sir ; I have been in these parts, and my character"—

" Silence, John Jones !—answer my questions. I repeat, you are a native, and have lived in this village for a considerable time ?"

I have ; and you know, sir, as how I wouldn't do wrong."

" Silence, again," said the lawyer ; " I know no one in my professional capacity. To me you are as a myth. You are a stranger."

John Jones, now more than ever convinced this was the prelude to some dreadful crime, for which he was to be denounced, turned very pale, and his bulky figure was seen to tremble, whilst Lawyer Crawsuit feeling naturally a weakness to which we of the human mould are prone, like the cat and the mouse, rose six feet higher in his own importance, and enjoyed the carpenter's perturbation with a thousand-fold stronger relish.

" You are now, sir, erecting a greenhouse adjacent to or near my house ?"

" I be, sir," was the reply.

" You have been at work on that greenhouse this morning ?"

" Ye—es, your honour !"

"Do you usually wear a paper, otherwise a parchment, cap when labouring at your calling?"

"I do, sir."

"And is this the cap aforesaid?"

"That be the cap, sir," answered the carpenter, scratching his head in amazement.

"Now, sir," continued the lawyer, "I appeal to you, as the father of a family, as the husband of a wife, if you have one spark of that divine instinct called Christian charity; if your heart is not like Lot's wife, turned into a pillar of stone—I mean salt; if your bosom contains one germ of fellow-feeling for suffering humanity, answer me truthfully, for the welfare of the poor of the parish depends on your reply; where, where, did you obtain this cap?"

Overcome by his exertions, the orator sank back into his chair, whilst the meaning of the exhortation became addled in the brain of John Jones to a confused mass of words, of which the only part he understood was, that the happiness of the poor folks depended, somehow or other, on his old dirty cap.

"No equivocation: I await your reply," said the lawyer,

"Well, sir, this be all a mystery to I; but I'll tell thee how I come by it; there be no harm as I knows on. I got it out of Lawyer Quirk's dusthole. When he died, thee knows, the house was turned inside out, and amongst the rubbish as wasn't burnt, was that there bit of parchment, which was swept up with other muck, and was pitched into the dust heap. So says I to my mate, says I, 'Comrade, this here would make a slap-up waterproof cap.' 'Yes, says he.' So, says I, 'Blow'd if I don't take it home,' And so I did, and makes one on't; it's lasted I ever since, mayhap some seven or eight years. That's the truth, sir, as I'm a sinner."

"Good heavens!" ejaculated the lawyer—"strange, very strange!—a wonderful cap—an interposition of Providence! Enough, my man. I will give you a sovereign for it, nor is that all you will receive."

"What! for my old cap? Tak' it and welcome, your honour. I wishes I had another, at the same price. Bless your honour! Good morning."

Both parties then separated, well pleased with the bargain—John Jones to wonder and speculate over all the virtues discovered in his cap, and the lawyer to commence proceedings against the squire for the recovery of the field left by his predecessor, to the poor, the cap being the identical deed of gift which had been missing. Not long elapsed before the new squire, much to his chagrin, was not only compelled to surrender it, but also to pay a handsome rentage as compensation for the years of his unjust occupation. Mr. Lawyer Crawsuit was ever afterwards acknowledged the great and presiding genius of the village. New clients came in; Mrs. Crawsuit now rested proudly on her laurels, to the discomfiture of the Pimple family; her childlessness was to her no longer a reproach; henceforth "her family were the poor." This she told Mrs. P., with upturned eyes, and a solemn voice. Mrs. P. could not deny it, and effectually was silenced.

The poor subscribed one shilling each, and gave a feast in honour of John Jones, the carpenter, at the Cat and Fiddle. The said worthy, in acknowledging the vociferous applause which greeted the proposal of his health, did as thousands of his betters do—returned thanks in prosy unintelligible jargon, bringing, however, his harangue to a termination with flying colours, by proposing the following toast: "Ladies and gents, all, I hopes as how you'll have another gallon at my expense, to drink—confusion to the squire as is living—a loving cup to the memory of him as is dead—and God's blessing on my wonderful Old Parchment Cap!"

SHATTERED HOPES.

"Pale as he is, here lay him, lay him down,
O lay his cold head on my pillow;
Take off, take off these bridal weids,
And crown my careful head with willow.

Pale tho' thou art, yet best, yet best beluv'd,
O could my warmth to life restore thee;
Yet lye all night between my breists,
No youth lay ever there before thee.

Return, return, O mournful, mournful bride,
Return, and dry thy useless sorrow;
Thy luver needs none of thy sighs,
He lies a corpse in the Braes of Yarrow."

PERCY'S RELIQUES.

At the door of a respectable house in the good old cathedral city of ——, there stood two hired conveyances one delightful morning in the month of April, 1852. The drivers, by their brilliant white cotton gloves, their highly-polished boots, and the flowers they wore in their coats, were evidently arranged for the purpose of doing honour to some momentous event. Their bearing, too, bore unmistakeable signs of importance. Familiarity with the crowd was entirely at an end, for the present, and the curious inquisitive glances of the youngsters, with the cunningly-put interrogatories of the gossip-loving women, were alike treated with silent disdain. So matters stood for about half an hour, the tedium of which was only relieved by sundry boxes on the ears bestowed on a few dirty little urchins, who ventured to overstep the bounds of good behaviour, by endeavouring to peep through the keyhole of the door before which the conveyances were stationed, or make mud pies on the door steps. At length a head appeared over the blinds of one of the lower windows. Some telegraphic signals were exchanged—expressive to the bystanders as the nod of Lord Burleigh in "The Critic"—and the chariot doors and steps were instantly lowered. There was a general crowding amongst the lookers-on. A cry of "They're coming," then a quarrel between two women, and a fight between two boys, each accusing the other of "shoving," and a bridal party descends—all modest blushing tremor, innocent vanity, or transient happiness. They jump into the coaches, crack go the whips, and away they drive to connect the firmest and most eventful link in all that great chain of which the life of two individuals is composed.

Need we journey with them to the altar? No, I think not, reader; for it is more than probable you have taken part in that interesting ceremony—

once, twice, perhaps thrice in your life—and therefore know all about it; it would be an old tale hardly worth telling, except to those longing, hoping, fearing young ladies who think, and live, and dream of nothing else but to realize such an occasion, and who, when the occasion has passed, look too often in vain for the romance which their own ideal natures conjured up. To such a class, I am well aware, the very description of the dress would be a source of deep interest; however, suffice it for us to know there was the usual amount of tears expended, the usual blushes, the usual awkwardness, and the usual congratulations after it was over. The signatures and other matters were settled in the vestry, the clergyman wished them happiness, buttoned up his pocket with the fee in it, and departed; the clerk followed in the footsteps of his superior, the sexton and pew-opener did the same, and the happy party returned, to the infinite delight of the little boys and girls who had by this time transferred their favours and amusements from the door step to the gutter.

Were I writing for a newspaper I should, in announcing such an event, fall back upon those ever-memorable and never-deviating characteristic descriptions to which the reporters of this country are attached—"hymeneal altar"—"lovely and accomplished"—"happy pair," etcetera; but being a private individual personally accountable to the reader for the truth of my tale, I am content with less aspiring terms, and in place of "lovely and accomplished," insert the more humble but decidedly more suitable acquisitions for a good wife of "pleasing, affectionate, and domesticated," for such in every sense the lady I speak of was—one of three sisters who had been left to struggle on together, with a mere existence at their hands, but that existence was raised by them into a respectable and honoured position, thanks to their innate virtues, perseverance, and self-respect. Of these three the bride of the day was the eldest—about nine-and-twenty—who had, by the advice of her well-wishers, accepted the offer of marriage from a Captain Western, a good-looking manly young commander of an East Indian trader, a native of the place, and but twenty-seven years of age.

A fortnight passed over with the usual amount of happiness attending such a period, when the long vista of the future is obscured by the silver cloud of love and novelty attending the days of our honeymoon. At the end of that time their felicity was brought to an abrupt termination by a mandate from Captain Western's employers that he should immediately resume command of his ship, it having been chartered by government to sail within a few days, carrying troops to the East, and from thence, on account of the firm, to sail for Australia. Under these circumstances nothing was left but an instant separation for a long, very long period. The parting on both sides was a sad one, as can well be imagined, more so, perhaps, on the part of the wife, she knowing how many dangers must beset her husband's path 'ere they again should meet. The moment came!—the last kiss was given, the good bye spoken, and the young man left his wife standing on the pier at Gravesend, to which place she had accompanied him. It was a glorious morning; she watched the white sails unfurl—she regretted her words had been so few, but at such a moment the voice is apt to fail, the tongue refuses its office, and the longing, lingering gaze becomes the only exponent of the bursting heart. Thus she stood, heedless of the poor soldiers' wives who, like herself, were suffering the greatest of their earthly trials—heedless, too, of the poor children who had looked their last upon their fathers. When the vessel disappeared beyond the horizon then she left the spot, and taking the earliest train returned home to take her first lesson in the use of that hard and bitter antidote called *patience*.

Time in its resistless course had swept nearly two years away, and found Mrs. Western looking forward to her husband's return. Letter after letter had reached her, tracing his course from one great distance to another. On the passage to Australia the ship had been, by a miracle as it were, saved from destruction in a fearful storm encountered. Some of his crew were washed overboard, others were disabled, and by dint of unremitting toil and anxiety he had reached Melbourne—the vessel completely worthless, his cargo nearly all lost, and himself invalided by his severe sufferings. Through instructions he received from his employers in London, on recovering from his sickness he left for England in another of their homeward-bound vessels, commanded by a friend. This fact was notified to Mrs. Western in his last letter, and his arrival was to be expected within about a week of Christmas-day. During the interval of his absence, I need hardly say all Mrs. Western's thoughts had been centred on the event of his return. Her marriage-dress had been carefully and religiously preserved for the sole purpose of wearing it in his sight again; not a walk—not a visit—not a pleasure that the most loving heart could wish or plan, but she had thought of. Clothes, too, of all descriptions were prepared for him—all of them the labour of the long weary months she had passed—and as the time drew near, months had been counted into weeks, weeks into days, and days into hours.

At length came a letter, written almost within

sight of England. Every word bespoke the pleasure he anticipated in the meeting, and after enumerating heaven only knows how many Indian and Australian treasures he was bringing her, concluded thus:—"We are within two days' sail of the Downs should the wind keep fair: meet me in London on Tuesday next, at the same place we stayed at on our last visit. For God's sake come, my darling! I so long to see you, and cannot wait until I reach ——; bless its old cathedral towers, I see them now, with you at my side. Heaven be thanked, in a few days it will be so—'till then I remain your loving and devoted husband,

"ROBERT WESTERN."

On receipt of this a few necessaries were got ready, and on the Monday morning Mrs. Western started for London on her joyful errand, leaving endless instructions behind her as to the changes and preparations necessary for her husband's comfort on his arrival, and above all, those appertaining to the Christmas-day, when a family gathering was to give him a welcome home.* Arriving in London, she hastened to the address of their

---

* It was the night following Mrs. Western's departure for London I took apartments in her sister's house, being strongly recommended there by a friend, and thus became cognizant of this sad episode of life.

former lodgings, which happened to be in the heart of the city. The first night passed over, and the morning dawned when she might expect his coming. A dull fog hung like a thick pall over the metropolis, and a drizzling rain fell through the entire day—dim sickly-looking lights struggled through thickly grimed and painted windows from rooms where countless thousands were bartered for—dense columns of smoke just rose above the thousand chimneys, then fell in showers of blacks upon the heads of the busy people hurrying to and fro in the streets, or lodging upon the windows, and nooks and crevices of the houses, adding to their begrimed and uninteresting appearance. From earliest dawn, waggons laden with the produce of every quarter of the globe—from the sunny regions of the south, or the ice-bound north, rumbled along; whilst lighter vehicles in their ceaseless rattle completed the din of London life. All these strange sights and sounds were alike unheeded by the anxious lonely watcher—she had eyes but for one object now—to look on her husband—ears but to listen for the fall of his feet upon the stairs; and so hoping and listening she passed from chair to window, and from window to chair, till morning, afternoon, and at length night fell once more upon the busy world at her feet. Then the noise without subsided, leaving a thousand-fold stronger sense of loneliness upon her heart. In this vast city she found a pang of utter solitude, which was intensified and increased by the knowledge of the wondrous life around her. Not so feels the sorrow-stricken wanderer in the midst of green fields, flower-studded hedgerows and noble trees, for there he has an inward assurance that God is watching over him—it is whispered to him in the glorious beauty of his surrounding works—in every passing breeze, in the melody of every bird, in the blue sky, in the twinkling of the stars. Consolation such as this is lost in the filth, the bustle, the choking atmosphere, the crime, and the drunkenness af a great city. Wearily the long hours of the night passed, and again dull morning broke, without bringing her ease, but towards noon a letter, written in a strange hand, was given her: it ran as follows:—

"Deal.

"Dear Madam—I am sorry to inform you your husband is suffering from an accident he unfortunately met with. On receipt of this, I should advise your immediate departure from London, for this place. You will find him at the enclosed address. Yours very obediently,

"JOHN MARTIN."

By the first train Mrs. Western started for

Deal. As the train passed on its way, swift as was its speed, it could not keep pace with the quick impatient throbbings of her heart; she envied every bird that glided past with swifter wing. The lights of Deal came at length in view—people wondered at her anxious looks and nervous gestures; had they known the feelings which prompted them, their wonder must have turned to pity. The noisy convulsive puffings of the mighty engine became more measured, a shrill and startling whistle broke on the night air, and the train stopped. On Mrs. Western alighting, she looked around in vain for her husband—for despite the information conveyed in the letter, it is sometimes hard to believe or credit "the messenger of ill," and hope tenaciously clung that he might be there to meet her. On not finding him, the first sudden horror of a certain impending calamity shot like an arrow through her brain—the blow seemed indefinite, but fearfully intense—it sent her blood with a chill through every vein. Calling a coach, she ordered the man to drive with all speed to the address she had received.

It was not more than ten o'clock, an hour in London when the dissipation of life is barely commenced—when from courts and alleys (which are as numerous as arteries in the body of some monstrous Megalosaur) come—or rather crawl—

the diseased and sin-stricken multitude, to hide their misery or excite their sluggish blood in mad riot, secret crime, and drunken debauchery; but here in the dear, quaint old towns of England, such as Deal, at ten o'clock a quiet reigns more profound than the great Babylonian capital can boast of in any hour of the twenty-four. So through the silent streets the coach wheels rattled, in their echo seeming to wake the strange shadows of grim spectres that started out from the dark nooks, and corners, and crevices of the old-fashioned houses. The driver stopped at last before a clean-looking inn of modest but respectable pretensions. He knocked at the door, and the landlady, a good, clean, motherly-looking old soul, who had evidently been anxiously waiting Mrs. Western's arrival, came out, assisted her guest to alight, and discharging the coach conducted her with great consideration and kindness to a small private room. Once there, Mrs. Western sunk into a chair, and gazed with imploring yet fearing eyes full upon the face of the conductress. Not a word was spoken for a minute or so, but gradually an expression of the most profound sympathy and sorrow spread over the old woman's face, and big tears came rolling down her cheeks. For a time the young wife looked on in imploring agony, burning, yet fearing to ask, until at last came forth the terrible words—

"For God's sake tell me where is my husband?"

"I cannot say, madam—I cannot say, at least he be very ill!"

"Ill, and I not at his side? Oh! feel for a wife's anguish and tell me."

"I do, poor lassie, I do. Dear, dear-e me, what shall I say—I would that my old man wer here, he'd tell thee better ner me." The old woman sat herself down and rocked to and fro, at an apparent loss for words to express her feelings or give utterance to the secret.

"Woman! woman!" cried Mrs. Western, "feel for me as for yourself; I am prepared to hear the worst—and do not fear it—anything is better than this suspense."

"Ay, Ay, but I'm an old woman; I've had my sorrows, but none so bad as this—but it were better told perhaps—he met with an accident."

"What was it?—where is he?"

"I'm coming to it, lassie—too soon for thee, I fear. He met with a fall, you see, and he hurt his poor back. The doctor thought at first there were not so much the matter: then they brought him here."

"Here, here! in this house, and I sit talking like this! Oh, take me to him; the very sight of me, I know, will make him better."

"I fear me not! I fear me not! The sight of thee will hardly gladden his poor eyes again."

"Oh, God help me! Tell me, do you mean he is dead?"

"The Lord's will be done! I canna tell thee that; have courage, and I'll take thee where he is."

She then took the candle from the table, and led the way up a narrow flight of stairs. Mrs. Western followed with almost unconscious steps up the first landing, when the landlady paused, looked back with a troubled face, and said, "The Lord's will be done! it may be for the best; have courage will 'ee."

"I will, I will, I am prepared, mother; now go on."

The old woman then laid her hand on the door facing the stairs, and turning the handle opened it. At that moment a gust of wind coming through the open lattice extinguished the candle, and she, with a scream, started back with fright; but the heart of the wife found no room for fear: when she beheld in the pale beams of the moon a white motionless object, stark, and human-like, outstretched upon the bed, she rushed towards it, and instinctively drawing aside the sheet, beheld the beloved features of her husband fixed in death before her, looking ghastly and terrible in the lambent rays from heaven. Far, far upon the night breeze arose a fearful shriek; the wayfarer as he trod the streets of Deal shuddered as he heard it, and many paused upon their way to know its meaning; but in vain! It came—it passed away. The town and its inhabitants still slept, unmindful, and uncaring for a sister's sorrow.

The people of the inn rushed up stairs—all there was silence now—the living had but fainted on the bosom of the dead.

It appeared that two days previously, whilst smoking a cigar and stepping towards a boat to land, he turned to make some jocular remark to a friend, when his foot slipped, he fell back, and died within a few hours from the effects. Thus, though he had passed over thousands of miles and escaped so many dangers, the grim spectre seized him when apparently most secure.

Oh! wise, wise Hamlet!

"If it be now, 'tis not to come; if it be not to come, it will be now, yet it will come: *the readiness is all.*" "There's a divinity that shapes our ends, rough—hew them how you will."

AN IRISHMAN'S DOUBLE.

In the year 1795, a trial took place in Paris which created considerable interest, from the respectability of the accused person, a Monsieur Lesurques.

A courier when in charge of the mail was murdered one evening at Lieursaint, and upon the evidence of most creditable witnesses, Monsieur Lesurques was sworn to as being the assassin; besides which, a string of most singular coincidences occurred to warrant the truth of the accusation. He was tried—found guilty, and a fatal stroke of the guillotine consummated the lamented error of justice; for it was afterwards discovered that the executed man was perfectly innocent of the crime, and the true murderer was a notorious robber—between whom and Monsieur Lesurques there existed the most marvellous resemblance in face, height, voice, and indeed every particular except virtue.

THANKS to Mr. Charles Kean, many people are acquainted with the above facts from the English dramatic translation of "The Courier of Lyons;" and this must be considered as only one instance of the many where mistaken identity has brought upon the innocent misery, shame, and death. When we reflect upon the probability of error in all circumstantial evidence, however clear that evidence may appear, does it not seem that capital punishment never in such cases should be resorted to ?—better that the guilty should escape than the innocent suffer. At all times death is a fearful alternative, coldly and deliberately to prepare, by means of prayer and good living—(that is, if the poor wretch be able to eat)—a fellow-creature, and then to lead him forth to slaughter, like a fatted calf, gratifying by his last convulsive struggles thousands of eager and wicked hearts, whose eyes and thoughts revel in the morbid horror of such a sight. As an instance of the almost incredible callousness to which vice may reduce our natures, and the utter uselessness of such exhibitions to impress a fearful lesson upon the criminal offshoots of society—I recollect a circumstance that occurred at Bristol, on the occasion of a young girl being hanged for beating her mistress's brains out with a stone. (The circumstances of this murder may still be remembered, from the coolness and systematic manner in which the horrible crime was perpetrated, as also from the fact of the murderess, with the corpse at her feet, cooking pancakes and concocting other luxuries to enjoy herself with. The execution of this girl, too, made some noise at the time, in consequence of her determined resistance—she being actually dragged from the cell on to the scaffold, with the most appalling screams. Thus the rope was fastened round her neck, and in this state she was launched into eternity—a murderess certainly, but to my mind, judging from all the particulars of the case, an undoubted maniac also.)

On the morning of these occurrences, I was walking along one of the narrow dirty thoroughfares of Bristol, to make a short cut into Wine street, when a slatternly girl of about seventeen attracted my attention, leaning against a door. Another female was passing at the time, to whom the creature shouted—" I say, Sue, are you going to see our Sal tucked up this morning?" in about the same tone as one would invite the other to a wild-beast show.—This was the murderess's sister. However deserving of death the culprit may be, as it is utterly impossible, as in the case of the girl just spoken of, for us to have power against the will over the soul, and force repentance, so is it with me a serious doubt that we are empowered by any law, human or divine—to plunge a fellow-creature into eternal damnation, or even, should he repent, to usurp the authority of God by holding the balance of life and death. If positively guilty I would not have them let loose upon society. Treat them as wild beasts, cage them: death is mercy; let the criminal, shut from all human sympathy, feel the anguish of a remorse that must one day come. The upholders of such judicial proceedings may quote Scripture to further their ends, but I, as an opponent, could equally do so: besides which, there is scarcely a creed extant, however monstrous in its docrines, but its professors may and do lay their fingers on a text and distort it to suit their purposes.

I have been led into this train of thought by the sad fact heading this sketch inducing the contemplation of crime and its punishment, together with the chance of mistaken identity as further illustrated by the circumstances I am about to relate, and for the truth of which I am able to vouch.

I was sitting by the fire at my lodgings, in a town situated in the southern portion of England, and happened to be in a very bad humour; for that bane to every bachelor's life, "a washerwoman," had disappointed me, and was a fortnight behind her time in returning the last bundle of linen with which she had been entrusted. It was on this occasion the more to be regretted, as not having much with me my stock had run short, and I was invited out to meet a few friends and strangers, under circumstances which rendered clean linen rather indispensable. Whilst sitting thus in moody silence, inwardly vowing vengeance against the delinquent washerwoman, a knock came to the door. "Come in," I shouted—and in walked the very individual. "So you have ccme at last, Mrs.

Murphy; what the deuce do you mean by keeping my clothes all this time? Really it is too bad; I shall employ somebody else, or you will be the death of me, I feel convinced. "Plaize yer honour to look over it this once," said Mrs Murphy, in a whining tone. "'Once,' what do you mean by 'once?' this is the second time in a few weeks. You will ruin me, woman!"

"Plaise yer honour, I couldn't help it."

"Couldn't help it! Nonsense!" I replied, growing more indignant; "that is just what you said when you thrust the iron through my shirt-front the last time you brought the things home. That is what you all say when I complain of the gradual and incessant disappearance of my buttons. I wonder you have not more feeling for a man without a wife."

"An' sure it's sorry I am; but if ye'll jist look over it this once; I've been in mighty throuble, an' that's the thruth on't. I was a going to axe yer honour, if ye'd be plaised to listen and give me a bit of advice, for, ochone! it's sad my heart is now, anyway."

"It's more than you deserve," I replied, somewhat mollified by the tears I saw gathering in the poor woman's eyes; "Ill listen, and do the best I can for you. Go on."

However well we may be acquainted with the

usual insincerity of "Irish blarney," and the ever ready commodity it is, whereby to purchase the smallest favour with, yet is there a something peculiarly insinuating in the tone and manner of its delivery, that whilst feeling ourselves humbugged we submit—so on this occasion. I did not, however, regret my amiability and patience, but found myself repaid by the singularity and truth of the woman's story. Thus it ran :—

"You must know that Mike—that's my husband, yer honour—some few years ago was as honest a lad as ever confissed his sins to the blessed Father Maguire or ate pratees; but times got very bad: for weeks poor Mike was out of work, and all that time we had to live upon the bit o' washin' I could get—an' little enough it was to support two grown up people an' two little childers; but there was no help, so I said, "Thy will be done!" But not so, Mike: he took on sadly, for he was always a good lad, an' had a kind heart, yer honour. He didn't like to see me a-workin' my flesh to the very bones to get the bit an' the sup. You see, I thought that times would mind when the sunshiny weather came in, but they got worse instead of betther, an' the pratees got so scarce an' dear that many a night we took to our beds wid empty stomachs and aching hearts. Well, sir, one night I had been sitting all alone, looking at the two or three bits o' coal as was a-burnin' in the fire-place which I had picked up in the streets, a wishin' for Mike to come home and warm hisself before they quite went out, and it's wonderin' I was what kept him so long, when I hears his footsteps on the stairs. He came into the room lookin' so white and scared that all my blood went cold; he was carryin' a basket full of bread an' pratees an' meat, besides which he showed me in his hand some bright shinin' pieces of goold. Instead of feelin' happy at the sight of thim I felt ten times more miserable than I was afore, for I knew the boy had been and done wrong. I axed him where they came from, and he tould me to 'niver mind but be contint, that I shouldn't be afther bein' hungry niver any more.' Then he said, 'A frind, who wished to save us from starvation, had sent it.' So I tried to think it was all right, for Mike had niver desaved me: and we had the bit an' the sup an' went to bed. But it was heavy, somehow, my supper lay upon my conscience that night—not a wink of sleep could I get, or Mike either, which made me feel all the worse: so it's glad I was to see the morning a-breaking, for then I prayed that my fears might not prove thrue; but, ochone, ochone! jist at that moment came a loud knockin' at the street door. Mike jumped out of bed as if he'd been shot; 'For the love of God, Betty,' said he, 'don't let them in, or I'm ruined intirely.'

" 'Who are they, Mike,' said I; 'What had you been afther doin' that you should be so scared?' 'Don't ax me; the divil tempted me an' hunger made me do it. They're coming up stairs; oh, what'll I do! what'll I do—it's mad I shall go.' Well, yer honour, the next moment the room was filled with the perleece; I thried to save him, and tould thim it was hunger as made him stale. I offered all the things back, but it wer no use; they dragged him away, put him in prison, and oh! it's heavy my heart wer then, anyway. Many a time I walked round an' round the big, cruel shtone walls in the hopes of seein' him; but it were no use—he was tried, found guilty of breakin' into another man's house an' stalin', an' he was sintenced to ten years' transportation. Whilst he was a being tried I stood in the coorthouse hopin' to cheer the poor lad, by a-smilin' at him, but I could see the big large tears a-comin' into his eyes; and when they sintenced him, it's scream I did, and faintin' away, was carried out o' the coort. I got home at last, an' sat for many a-day a cryin' and keenin whilst the childers wer starvin'; when I thought o' this I made up my mind to set to an' do a something—so I went about from house to house 'till I got work. Ah, sure, sir, it's many a man before Mike that an empty stomach or starvin' wife and childers have made a thief of. You who have plenty may talk of contintment, but it's hard to feel it, when you crave a bit of bread, whilst others have more nor enough and give what would satisfy the hunger to their dogs; but the Lord presarve you from feelin' the temptation.

"Abont two years afther Poor Mike had been gone, a letther was put into my hand by the postman. It came from Ireland, an' said that an aunt of mine in the ould counthry was dead, an' she'd left me her fortune—which was one hundred pounds. Oh thin sure, wasn't it glad I was, and didn't I fancy myself the richest woman in all the world—its pray I did, to the Holy Virgin an' all the blessed saints to send Mike back to me, soon; but it wer all o' no use, so I thoucht I'd sit myself down an' wait patiently—an' I took a house an' lit lodgings, afther I had furnished it beautiful from top to bottom. I still did a bit in the washin way o'course, to save all I could against the boy's coming back. Five years had gone, when about six months ago who should I see sittin by the fire one night when I came home—a'smokin his pipe, an lookin as happy as ever he did in the ould days—but Mike! Oh sure, bad luck to me! for its run into his arms I did—an' its mighty hard he squeezed me with joy; then I looked at him—he was a bit browner maybe in the face, an' I thoucht him a little taller—sartain sure his clothes wer shabbier; but that was easily accounted for—thim's all the alterations I could see, an' its happy we two wer that evenin anyhow. He tould me he had got a ticket-of-lave for his good conduct, so we had a very happy chat, 'till I told him of my good fortun, an' its then beside hisself wid joy he was. For the fust few weeks he seem'd kinder ner ever, and thin he changed; kept bad company—got roaring dhrunk all night, and went to bed to get hisself sober agin in the day. My lodgers he frightened away; he spent all my money as fast as I could get it, an' the deuce a bit o' work would he do. He said he was a gintleman, an' he'd spend his money like one; so he did, for in five months all my fortune and the hard earnings of many a weary day was gone. My only hope was when he'd got no more money he'd go an' lave me; but no—he sould all my beautiful furniture, to the very bed we had under us; an' one night I came home tired enough after takin home some washin, an' its find I did he'd been and sowld my wash tubs, the only thing I'd lift to keep body an' soul together; so I was lift without a penny or the manes of gettin one. Some kind ladies an' gintlemen subscribed to set me on my legs agin, and och sure, its fearful I was he'd come back! It's many a big tear I dropped to think he'd behaved so cruelly to me, afther the days an' nights an' months of watchin, sorrowin, an' workin I'd gone through for his sake: but, thinks I, the childers mustn't starve—so I sits to work agin, and when I felt the big tear come up from my heart, enough to choke me, I says, 'Mavourneen, Mavourneen,' an' sent it down agin. Well, may-be a week ago I'd been assistin a lady to clane her home, an' feelin very tired, I opened my room door, when who should I see sated in the very chair a-smokin his pipe, but Mike, jist as I'd seen him afore. It's then for the fust time in my life the divil came into my sowl, an' I thoucht I could kill him.

"'Ah, Betty, my jewel, an' it's there ye are,' said he—'an bless ye, darlin!'

"Bad luck an' the divil fly away wid yer,' said I, seizin a stool, the first thing that came to hand. 'Kape off! kape off! or it's hanged I'll be for murtherin you, if ye don't kape out o' this house.'

"'Why, Betty, yer dreamin, sure; don't yer know me?'

"'I do, ye blackguard; ye've ruined me once, an' now ye've come back to ruin me agin.'

"'An' sure, Betty, I niver ruined ye in all my life. The Lord presarve us, she's gone mad!' he cried, starin at me so quare.

"'Mad!' said I, 'it's not your fault that I'm

not—ochone ! it's miserable I am, any way ; it's many a long day I sat in this very room, a-waitin yer comin back—an' I counted the hours almost, afther I got my big fortun, an' says I to myself—'When Mike does come back, poor boy, its repay him this will for all his sufferin.' Just thin, Mike got up and put his hand on the wash tub—'No, yer don't,' says I, layin hold of it—'yer sowld the others, but ye shall drag me away wid these afore I'll part wid 'em ; lave me the manes to get the bit an' the sup for the childers, an' I'll forgive yer, though you've spent my fortun, and sowld all my beautiful furniture. Mike, it's love yer once I did, an' I niver thoucht the day would come when I should curse ye ; had ye been an honest lad now, as you were when I fust knew yer, it's happy we might have been wid my money which you've dhrunk.'

"'I dhrunk yer money, Betty ? What the divil do yer mane by yer fortun ? By my sowl it was a mighty small one, any-way ; for I niver knew you had one afore, except a bright silver saxpence, which yer grandfather gave ye on our weddin day.'

"It's now I began to wondher—for he didn't seem dhrunk—an' he spoke so much more like the Mike of my heart than he that sowld me up, so I axed him if he didn't ruin me a short time back ? An' he swore by the blessed St. Patrick he'd niver set eyes on me afore, since he was on his trial. Then I felt scared, for I thoucht I must have been livin' wid his ghost or the ould gintleman hisself who had taken Mike's shape to rob me of my sowl. Jist as I was a thinkin', Mike jumps up in a mighty big passion, lookin' as white as thim shirts; says he, 'Och, sure, bad luck to me, I see it all.' An' thin he up an' towld me that some months afore he had his ticket-of-lave another Irishman workin in the same gang, whom they called Pat Sweeney, had got his,—that they were as much alike as two paes in a pod,—so much so that they were always bein' mistaken one for the other; Pat was a bit taller, that were all. Well, when Pat got his ticket, Mike had towld him where to find me out, an' all about me, for they were friends, an' Mike thoucht him an honest lad, who like hisself had fallen into bad ways from poverty; so he axed him to come and see me an' comfort me, an' Pat promised him, 'for the sake o' the ould counthry, he'd do it.' An,' says poor Mike, 'it's comfort ye he has wid a vengeance.' 'Ochone! Mike dear, "said I," what'll I do, what'll I do; I couldn't help it.'

"'But did he live intirely wid yer, Betty, like myself?'

"'An' sure he did, Mike; but I thoucht it was you all the time.'

"'It's a robbed and murthered man I am altogether, then,' cried poor Mike. 'Oh, Betty, you've been an' gone an' committed burglary by livin' wid anoder man: Oh, the bla'guard! let me catch him an' its bring him to justice I will.'

"An' it's what we'll do to find him out; maybe yer honour might tell us, for it's mad I've been ever since as any livin' sowl in this breathin' world: an' as for poor Mike, he's a great deal madder.'"

Making every allowance for the simplicity of the woman's nature, this is certainly an extraordinary instance of the similarity which may exist between two human beings.

THE LIFEWRECK.

Alas! our young affections run to waste,
Or water but the desert; whence arise
But weeds of dark luxuriance, tares of haste,
Rank at the core, though tempting to the eyes,
Flowers whose wild odours breathe but agonies,
And trees, whose gums are poison; such the plants
Which spring beneath her steps as Passion flies
O'er the world's wilderness, and vainly pants
For some celestial fruit, forbidden to our wants.

BYRON.

One of the chief ingredients made use of in the modern farce or comedy is the cool Jeremy Diddler impudence assumed by the chief male character, and this impudence, however amusing for the time being, conveys a strong smack of improbability about it to the minds of the many, they naturally believing such individuals are not to be met with in our every-day life, simply from the fact of their own immediate experience not having encountered them.

To prove that such astonishingly impudent men do exist to the perhaps sceptical reader, I relate the following somewhat unconnected facts respecting a young man whom it was once my misfortune to meet with. There is, however, a wide difference existing in the ideal *denouements* presented on the stage and that of real life. Old gentlemen are not to be met with who reward strange, eccentric, and worthless intruders with the hand of their lovely daughters, and a good round sum besides to keep matters square: such marvellous and imprudent acts of generosity confine themselves to the imaginative conceptions of the author, and the necessities of the actor's "situations," to use a technical phrase. My hero, therefore, following in the usual path allotted to indiscretion, found his young life wrecked on the shoals of dissipation, extravagance, and folly.

Some few years ago, I was walking up one of the streets in the town of Halifax, when I was accosted by a pale, light-haired, genteel-looking young man, apparently of not more than two-and-twenty. He was dressed in fashionably cut but exceedingly "seedy" clothes, and his hat bore unmistakeable evidence of a smash at no very distant period.

"Mr. Reeve, I believe I have the pleasure of addressing?" said this individual, whom we will call Royland; at the same time lifting his hat with an air *par excellence*.

"That is my name, certainly," I replied, looking rather shyly at his costume, "but to my knowledge I have not the pleasure of your acquaintance."

"I am sorry to contradict you, but you certainly have!"

"Indeed! I do not remember the circumstance."

"No! Well, that is surprising, too. I was introduced to you by B——, a mutual friend, in Derby, at a public dinner there; we had a cigar together."

"Oh, yes! I think I recollect your face now."

"Of course you do. B—— is a deuced nice fellow, only a little sharp after money when he lends it; that's his only fault, my dear sir."

"And I think that is a very necessary fault, in this fast age; for people do not generally run after you when they have borrowed money. But you really must excuse me, Mr.—Mr.—"

"Royland—Royland—but don't hurry yourself."

"I have a very particular engagement," said I, looking at my watch, as most people do when they want to get rid of a disagreeable acquaintance.

"You are going that way," he replied, pointing to the road I was about turning towards, "I have no particular destination at present; I shall be proud to bear you company."

"But, my dear sir—" I was about to tell him more plainly his society was not agreeable; before I could speak the words I found his arm linked in mine, as he said,—

"Not another word of apology, I beg; I am your most obedient for the rest of the day." Taken quite by surprise at the utter coolness of his conduct I suffered myself to be led through the streets by him. On observing his features more closely, I at once recalled the occasion of our first meeting. At the dinner he spoke of, I remembered remarking him for his gentlemanly, youthful, and self-possessed exterior, combined with a singularly insinuating and plausible impudence. On pointing him out to a gentleman, a friend by the name of B——, he informed me that the young man's name was Royland; he was connected with a highly respectable family near Manchester, and having at the age of seventeen inherited some property had run through a course of wild dissipation, and was then living upon the mere cipher that remained. He told me several anecdotes connected with him. One of these I transcribe:—

"Having been acquainted with his family some years, I have felt it my duty to receive him, but really his cool impudence surpasses all bounds. You must know, about three months ago, he arrived in Derby in a really miserable plight, having just finished up with some mad-headed 'spree,' to use his own term, and emptied his pockets of every farthing he possessed, or could possess, until a fresh supply arrived from the trustees. His clothes were half torn off his back, and as dusty as if he had been rolling in the road. In this state he called at my lodging, but I happened to be from home.

"'Not at home!' said he to my landlady, 'can you inform where I shall find him?'

"'Well, sir, I am not sure; but I think he went to meet a gentleman at the Royal Hotel.'

"'You think so, madam; thank you. If you will allow me, I'll walk upstairs and give myself a wash:' and away he started, pushing past the good lady to her infinite surprise. She not knowing what to do, seized on my great coat hanging in the hall, thinking his intention must be robbery. Having secured this she followed him up, and arrived just in time to have my bed-room door closed in her face and locked on the inside.

"'Sir, sir!' called out the good woman, knocking at the door, 'who are you?'

"'Who am I, madam? A gentleman—a friend of Mr. B——, whom I am about to pay proper respect to by having a wash. I require it, I can tell you, after the accident I have met with on the railway.'

"'Dear bless me: an accident! poor young man!' said the landlady, strongly sympathising with him, 'I hope you're not hurt, sir?'

"'No, no—not much—slightly bruised; but excuse me—I have an objection to be disturbed in my ablutions.'

"'Certainly, sir—I'll leave you;' and away went my landlady down stairs quite satisfied, the accident falsehood accounting for the visitor's strange appearance, &c.

"I had gone to the Royal, and was sitting with a friend talking over a little business, when Royland entered the room, dressed, as I thought, extremely well and looking very gentlemanly, his clothes not being unlike a suit of my own. 'Ah, B——, how do you do?' was the greeting; 'your friend here I have not the pleasure of knowing.'

"'Mr. Simpson,' said I, introducing him.

"'Most happy and proud of your acquaintance, Mr. Simpson; will you allow me the pleasure of wine or brandy-and-water with you, and a cigar?'

"'No, I thank you,' replied Simpson, to my satisfaction, 'I have some.'

"'But I insist—I'll hear no excuse,' urged Royland, loudly ringing the bell; 'waiter, bring us two brandies and cigars—a port as well; B——, I know that is your drink.'

"'A gentlemanly young fellow,' whispered Simpson to me. He happened to be a niggardly dog, and never paid if he could help it.

"'Two brandies, one port, and cigars,' said the waiter, placing the same on the table.

" 'A light,' cried Royland, selecting a cigar with great care.

" 'Yes, sir,' said the waiter, giving him one, and holding out the tray for payment.

" 'Ay,—what? Did you want anything?' he asked, looking with well-feigned surprise—first at the tray, then at the waiter.

" 'Brandies, cigars, and a port,' repeated that individual.

" 'Oh, yes, I see, you want the money; of course, very natural,' said Royland, as if the idea had just occurred to him—at the same time feeling with great energy in his pockets—'I am really afraid I have no change.'

" 'I can give you change,' cried Simpson.

" 'I thank you all the same—my turn another time. Waiter, go to that gentleman—he will pay you,' coolly replied Royland, pulling his hands out of his pockets, throwing himself back, and puffing away luxuriously at his cigar.

" 'I said I'd give you change,' bawled Simpson, evidently thinking him deaf.

" 'Exactly! happy to meet you, sir; pray do not keep the waiter—nothing less than a hundred pound note about me. Your good health, sir.'

" Had this occurred to any other individual, I certainly should have felt extremely annoyed; but having often experienced Simpson's meanness, on this occasion I rather enjoyed it, and pretended to be deeply immersed in the *Times* newspaper.

"'A great pity that young man is so deaf—really makes it very awkward; I have had to pay for these,' whispered Simpson to me.

"'Have you, indeed!—there is some mistake, surely,' I replied, and changed the subject. Shortly after this our friend took his departure, upon which I asked Royland about his present circumstances. The reply, as usual, displayed a continuation in a life of folly, carelessness, and dissipation. I gave him some excellent advice, and was very warm on the subject—he, getting a little excited, upset some brandy and water over the clean and handsomely worked front of the shirt he had on.

"'Confound it, that's a pity,' he said, rubbing it. It would have lasted me to-morrow.'

"'You are right, it is a pity," I remarked. 'It is very singular, I have a shirt exactly like that.'

"'Not at all singular, B——, it is your shirt, my dear boy; I've simply borrowed it!'

"'The devil you have! And the suit of clothes?'

"'All yours, I assure you. By the way, the trousers are a little too small for me round the waist. I was obliged to stretch them, and the stitches flew—nothing of any consequence. You can easily get them mended.'

"'Confound your impudence! How did you get them?'

" 'At your lodgings—don't be excited; it is easily explained. I have been on the spree for the last week—got into a row in the railway carriage with a man who objected to my putting my legs on the seat because my boots happened to rub against his coat, which I could'nt help; and with another, who said I should not smoke; then with the guard, because I couldn't find my ticket—the truth is I had no money to pay my journey, so determined to make them carry me without. I was obliged at last to give them a gold pin I had. All this bother did not improve my costume, and it certainly was not very bright before. Knowing you were a particular sort of fellow, I was really quite glad to find you were out; so thinking you might very probably feel annoyed at my rather seedy costume, I found everything I needed to transform myself into a gentleman, in your drawers—and here I am, my dear fellow. I was delighted, I assure you, to see you were pleased with my appearance when I entered; it was some recompense for the trouble of putting the things on, and studying your good opinion.'

" I need hardly say how much I was astonished and annoyed at this address. I expostulated with him strongly on the subject; but that only seemed to raise his surprise, for say what you like he never loses his temper or his impudence. I'll introduce you, only keep your eyes open." The introduction then took place. Such was the individual I found myself walking arm-in-arm with on the occasion of our meeting at Halifax.

"You are acquainted with a Mr. Martin of this town, are you not?" he inquired.

"Yes, I certainly know that gentleman."

"I have come down here for the purpose of assisting him—in fact I have made a short engagement with him professionally."

"Indeed, I was not aware"—

"That I understood his profession? Oh yes, I know a little about it. I have been recommended to him; but it is very unfortunate. You perceive my clothes are a little the worse for wear—effects of a railway accident."

"I am afraid you are rather subject to railway accidents," I remarked.

"Perhaps I am, a little; but this was a very sad one—you perceive it has smashed my hat. You have not half-a-sovereign about you, you could lend me to buy another?"

"I have not," I replied, decidedly.

"That is unfortunate, because it would have been of service. Never mind—is Martin given to lend money, do you know?"

"I am not aware that is one of his weaknesses."

"Do you think he will lend me a five-pound note?"

"As you are a stranger, I should be inclined to doubt it."

"But could not I offer you as security?"

"Certainly not; I am a stranger to you. I make it a rule never to be responsible even for a friend."

"That is unfortunate again. I'll talk to Martin, and show him the actual necessity for his own credit sake, as I am going to be with him. By the way you have a small foot, so have I: I think your boots would just fit me."

"I fear they would be too small."

"Too large—too large, you mean. You wouldn't mind lending me a pair until I have seen Martin, and borrowed five pounds of him?"

"You shall try a pair on," I replied, glad to purchase his absence, as I hoped, at such a sacrifice, and really feeling some degree of pity for the fellow when, on turning up his feet, I beheld the soleless condition of his shoes; besides this, I felt convinced my own would prove too small.

At length we arrived at my residence. I placed a pair before him. At these he tugged and tugged whilst my back was turned, until he split one of them up the back, much to my annoyance.

"It is of no use," he said, looking regretfully, "it is really a pity, for they would have suited me exactly—there is something rather stylish about the cut. You have not another pair, a little larger, have you?"

"No, I have not; at any rate, not for you to serve like this."

"You can easily get them mended, my dear fellow—will not cost you much; never mind. I'll go to Martin—good morning!" And away he started, to victimize that individual.

About a week after this occurrence I met Royland again, very handsomely dressed—French boots, light kid gloves, &c.—evidently the result of poor Martin's five pounds and the tailor's misplaced confidence.

"Well, how do you get on?" I asked, as he stopped in front of me.

"Tolerably—though really, Reeve, there is an amount of cool impudence about Martin I don't exactly understand."

"Indeed," said I, "he must be a clever man to teach you anything in that respect."

"You are mistaken, I assure you; my want of proper assurance has well nigh ruined me."

"Has it? I really should not have believed it had you not told me But what is the matter?"

"Why, in the first place I cannot get up before a reasonable time in the morning—say twelve o'clock; in the next, he objects to my taking a cup of chocolate and a cigar at four o'clock, because of people calling on business, or some nonsense of that sort; and lastly, he positively deducted, without consulting me, eight shillings this morning out of my salary, to go towards the liquidation of his paltry five-pound debt."

"Dear me, barbaric in the extreme! but what would you have him do?'

"Simply act in the manner of a gentleman, and wait until I offered it him.;'

"'Perhaps he thought he might wait long enough for that."

"Well it is, of course, probable that he might have to do so; but what of that? It would depend upon my liabilities, immediate and casual expenses, etcetera, etcetera.'"

After a few more words we separated, and I could but turn back to look after him and contrast his mild face and soft address, with the cool and daring effrontery of his nature.

Some months passed over, and I was staying in Manchester for a short time. One day I had been some little distance into the country, and returning rather late in the evening, to my great astonishment found Royland comfortably seated in my favourite arm-chair, smoking my meerschaum and reading a book. Being naturally of a civil and obliging nature, I did not turn him out, as I ought to have done, but simply remarking "he appeared to have made himself quite at home," sat down. In the course of conversation he informed me that he and Mr. Martin could not possibly agree—a fact I thought very easy of belief. Without being positively rude, I strongly hinted that his absence was more desirable than his presence. This however was entirely lost upon him; he sat with his legs stretched out, as though established for the night, so at length I thought it high time to retire and rising, said—"Well, Mr. Royland, you appear to be enjoying yourself, but I must beg of you to go; it is past my time of going to bed."

"Oh, well, don't mind me," was the reply.

"But, my dear sir, I am very tired."

"So am I, so am I—walked twenty miles to-day, with a sixpence in my pocket. Look at my boots."

I did look, and certainly wondered how he could possibly have surmounted a rough stony road with such wretched ones — they were indeed "the light of other days,"—being the French boots he had cut such a swell in at Halifax; that he had tramped from thence his condition was quite enough to prove. I could not help pitying him. "It is really very distressing that you do not guard against such suffering," I remarked; "you should be more careful when you have the means."

"Careful! my dear sir, there is no one more so, as far as the general feelings of a gentleman will permit. By-the-bye, what time is it?"

"Half-past one in the morning," I said emphatically.

"So early," was his reply—"dear me, I thought it was getting quite late! I am glad of that, there is just time to enjoy another pipe."

"You must excuse me, there is nothing of the kind; it is very late for me, at all events, and I am going to bed."

"You are? Well, what is to become of me?"

"Of you? My good fellow, I cannot say."

"Do you intend I should walk the streets all night?"

"I really cannot comprehend what I have to do with it. I am very sorry—but you have friends here, and I am not aware you possess any claim upon me."

"Yes, I have, my dear fellow—the claim of humanity and politeness. I have friends not very far off, it is true, but my disposition is opposed to theirs. If you turn me out, I must sleep on the door step, or place myself under the protection of the police—the first I only tried once, and found it infernally hard and uncomfortable."

"Well, sir," said I, deeply annoyed at being done in this manner—"I certainly cannot find it in my heart to 'turn you out,' as you call it—my landlady and the servant are gone to bed, but you can sleep in the adjoining room to mine for to-night."

"Thank you—I thought it would be all right—just oblige me with your slippers."

Not having a second pair, he had to go without, and perceiving his disinclination to move from the fireside, I turned out the gas—upon which he was obliged to follow me upstairs, where, bidding him good-night, we separted.

Morning came. At half-past eight I rose and knocked loudly at his door—then, dressing myself, went down stairs to await his rising for breakfast. Half-past nine struck, and no sign of my gentleman; going up stairs I walked into the room, and there he lay snoring. I called—it was no use—so handling him rather roughly compelled him at length to open his eyes.

"Is it you," said he, yawning; "don't bother a fellow in the middle of the night. D—n that sun, how it is shining—enough to put one's eyes out. Shut the shutters, Reeve, or I never shall be able to sleep."

"You have slept quite enough—I am waiting breakfast for you."

"Oh, don't mind me—I'll have mine in bed."

"Excuse me, my friend—but you certainly will have nothing of the sort. I think breakfasting in bed a most disgusting habit; so get up, or you will certainly go without any."

"Upon my soul, it is very hard a fellow cannot do as he likes. Well, I suppose I must, then," and he turned out with the air of a martyr.

At last he came down stairs, and casting his eyes on the breakfast table, seemed considerably disappointed.

"Don't you have chops for breakfast—I always do," was his remark.

"When you can get them, Royland, I suppose, and that won't be this morning; I dare say it is an oversight on my part, but you really must content yourself with what you see on the table." By some extraordinary stretch of endurance, he managed to clear all the toast, eggs, and bread and butter, then finished up with a biscuit.

"What time do you dine?" was his query, whilst swallowing the last mouthful.

"Very uncertain," I replied immediately; indeed the chances are, I shall not be at home to dinner at all to-day."

"Unfortunate; then I won't stay to dinner under those circumstances."

"No; I think you had better not.

Having an appointment, I, much to my gratification, got rid of this most unwelcome visitor. During that day and the next I heard no more of him, and was congratulating myself on the escape, when about twelve o'clock on the third evening a knock came to the door, steps were heard advancing towards my room, and in walked Royland, apparently a little gone in liquor, his face very pale, his eyes bloodshot, and his dress very disordered.

"Oh, my dear fellow, here I am—come to spend the night with you again—let me have a pull at—

"You are certainly a singular individual, Mr. Royland; we are comparative strangers, and I cannot accommodate you."

"Can you not? that is rather strange!"

"Not at all; you appear to labour under a strange delusion as to your conduct amongst friends and acquaintances."

"How so? I have done nothing, I trust, unbecoming a gentleman, Is the bed occupied?"

"It is."

"Oh, well, that is unfortunate, now—can I not share yours? I really do not mind."

"But I do. I have a great objection to anything of the kind."

"Have you? Well, I cannot tell why you should have; however—of course it is a bad job, we must make the best of it. Can you lend me half-a-sovereign?"

"No, I cannot,"

"Well—half-a-crown will do."

"I cannot lend you even that."

"Dear me, you must be very short! I like to serve a friend, for I know the annoyance of being so placed. I am aware that to the uninitiated it is no very agreeable task; but to serve a friend—I'll call again to-morrow. That is a capital coat of yours on the chair."

"Yes, it is a very good one," I replied, not seeing his drift.

"I'll pawn it for you, then you will not only be able to lend me five shillings, do you perceive, but you yourself will retain a larger sum. You can easily take it out again. Capital idea, that of mine."

This was a step, certainly, beyond all endurance, the idea of offering to pawn my coat in order to supply himself with money; so unable to control my temper longer, I gave him most unmistakeably to understand that he had better get out the same way he came in, or he might be helped by a quicker method. At this he professed the greatest surprise, and evinced the same in his manner, then coolly filled his pipe from my tobacco pouch, and looking upon me with an eye of pity, he marched out of the house.

Twelve months had probably now transpired and I had seen nothing of him, until the day of the York races, when the match took place between

Voltigeur and the Flying Dutchman—a day ever to be remembered in the annals of the race-course—and even to me, a novice in such matters, a time to be recollected with some degree of pleasure, from the thousands that were present—the marvellous excitement on the course, and the beauty of the animals, especially the Flying Dutchman. On the morning previous to the race, I remember seeing a pole at a barber's shop painted with Voltigeur's colours—white, if I recollect rightly, and red or a kind of crimson spots; by six o'clock two-thirds of the pole was painted a deep black—it was put "in mourning," as the barber said, for his losses, having half-ruined himself. This, however, is from the subject. In wandering round amongst the carriages, whom should I see but Royland—in an open landau, filled with gaily-dressed ladies of a particular class, and two or three rakish-looking men on the box, the whole party rioting with laughter, and handing champagne about by the tumbler-full, evidently at Royland's expense—he having the place of "honour?" in the body of the vehicle. He saw me, and beckoned, but I hurried off; and on encountering a gentleman a day or two after, with whom I knew him to be acquainted, I inquired the meaning of this, and was informed that by the death of a relation Royland had again become the possessor of several hundreds, which according to the present proceedings was calculated to last but a very short time. He further told me that he was killing himself rapidly. Every morning, to create an artificial spirit and power to endure the follies of the day, he had now accustomed himself to drink nearly a tumbler of raw brandy—without it he was nerveless—spiritless—almost dead. That very morning when I saw him in the carriage, previous to his rising from his bed, he had vomited nearly a pint of blood. Here was a picture of a young man between three or four and twenty, having possessed money, friends, health—everything calculated to make him happy—heedlessly destroying it all in the pursuit of a shadow which lured him fast and surely to the grave.

A few months only now passed away, and the same gentleman whom I encountered in Manchester gave me the following dreadful details.

"If you remember the day you spoke to me about Royland, I stated it as my opinion his constitution must sink under his excesses : it has done so. A week ago, the hour might be three in the morning, I was aroused by a loud knocking at the street door. On looking out of the window my ears were saluted by a female voice—the owner desiring to speak with me immediately. Utterly at a loss to comprehend what any female could want with me at that hour, I hesitated in complying, but was at length overcome by her earnest entreaties, so I dressed myself and went down stairs.

"'Do you know Mr. Royland, sir?' she inquired.

"'Yes; what of him?'

"'He is dying, sir; I'm sure he is. for God's sake come to him.'

"'Dying! Where?'

"'At a bad house, sir—the house where I live.'

"'Where you live? You, then, are—'

"'I am bad, sir,' she replied, interrupting me; but when I wish to do a kindness don't reproach me—I have some feeling of shame left yet.'

"'How am I to know you speak the truth?'

"'I have nothing but my word to give you, sir; but if you would assist the dying gentleman, that will be sufficient. I know few will believe a lost creature like myself; I swear to you I am speaking the truth now.'

"'How did you know he was acquainted with me?'

"'I once lived servant with his friends, sir; it was he who made me bad; that is all past now. I loved him then, and so it was my own fault.'

"There was a degree of earnest truth about the girl, despite her wretched appearance, which induced me to believe her; so, out of respect to Royland's relations I determined on seeing the prodigal. A few minutes sufficed for me to throw on a great coat, and to find myself following in the footsteps of my strange conductress through one of the most degraded and dirty streets of Manchester. After turning into an archway which conducted us into a filthy, narrow, and pestilential court, lit by a single lamp, hazy and dull in the thick atmosphere, we stopped before a poor and villanous tenement. I confess it was with some trepidation, and a tighter grasp of the stick I carried, I crossed the threshold. As we trod on the creaking stairs, an apparently drunken woman's voice cried out, 'Who the h—ll is that?'

"'Don't answer,' said my guide, 'it's only Poll; she's too drunk to make a row. Keep close to me or you may stumble.'

"Taking her advice we crept up stairs, to what appeared to be the second landing. Here my guide stopped, and listened at a door: 'I don't hear him now,' she whispered; 'wait a bit, I'll get a light.' Saying this, the girl dived into a crevice, to the right of where I stood, and left me to contemplate for a moment my anything but agreeable position, and conjure up all sorts of murders and robberies in such places, until I blamed myself severely for running the risk; however, such thoughts were at length dissipated by the girl re-appearing with a yellow, dirty-looking candle. I took it from her, quietly opened the door, and walked into the room, or rather den—for it was little better. Scarcely a particle of furniture was to be seen, the windows were rudely patched with paper and rags to keep out the wind, whilst obscene and gaudily-coloured pictures hung side by side with representations of our Saviour bearing the cross and other Scriptural subjects.

"Upon a foul bed I saw young Royland—his face white and attenuated—his hair matted and wild—his eyes fixed and glassy—with one arm supported by his hand, resting on a table at the side of the bed, on which stood a bottle half filled with gin, and a broken glass which he evidently had been reaching; the other hand clutched the hair of a young—once pretty—but dissipated-looking woman, who lay at his side, evidently overcome with intoxication, or, to speak more plainly, insensibly drunk.

"'Who is that?' I asked of the girl.

"'She keeps the house, and I know she has been robbing him. They came home drunk last night, and that woman was swearing because he said he was too ill to walk and felt sure he was dying. I thought he spoke the truth, he looked so strange and wild-like, his face quite frightened me, for I remembered him so good-looking; I crept upstairs and lay outside the door—until I heard them quarrel about the gin they had in that bottle—and then I heard blows; but presently all was quiet. I thought if he was to die like this, with no friend near him, how dreadful!—all at once I remembered hearing him speak of you, so I ran to your house.'

"'You did quite right; but I fear it is too late.'

"Going to the side of the bed, I caught hold of his hand. What was it that sent a thrill through my veins? I paused to think. I placed my hand upon his heart, and holding the candle, so as to throw its full light on his face, it disturbed the woman, who, with a muttered curse, turned round and slept, whilst a young life wrecked and wasted on the grave of passion slept beside her, to waken to other reckoning than *ours*."

A CHRISTMAS DINNER IN SCOTLAND.

With a good old fashion, when Christmas was come,
To call in all his neighbours with bagpipe and drum;
With good cheer enough to furnish every old room,
And old liquor able to make a cat speak, and man dumb,
Like an old courtier of the Queen's,
And the Queen's old courtier.

VERY OLD ELIZABETHAN BALLAD,
(Original of the "Fine Old English Gentleman.)"

WE have certainly degenerated in the hospitality observable at Christmas-time. It is no longer regarded in the same enthusiastic manner as of old; but I do sincerely hope, as it is, even in its present modified form, one of the last and best customs of the past, that the day is far distant when the feeling which still remains shall be altogether obliterated.

Through a long and severe struggle has it been maintained from the first century, when the Christians determined to observe, by rejoicing, the nativity of Christ. Though persecution in its most severe and barbarous form followed in their path, courageously they placed their feet upon the ladder of faith, and believed themselves securely shrouded by the wings of an all-powerful angel, choosing for the period of rejoicing the Saturnalia, when half the heathen population were mad with excitement. As to the correctness of the time in relation to the event it commemorated, there has been a great deal of dispute. Some of the old Greek authors maintain the 6th of April, others the 15th, 20th, and 25th of May. In 1722, in the Jesuit College of Rome, it formed the matter of considerable debate. In 1647 the parliament tried to abolish the observance altogether, which led to plenty of broken heads and the loss of a few lives; but from the time of the Restoration till the year 1752, the English people enjoyed undisturbed its privileges, then a squabble arose as to the right day being the 5th of January or the 25th of December. Those in the cause of the latter came off triumphant, and from that time to the present it has been the still recurring anniversary of warm hearts, loving eyes, joyful greetings, and family gatherings—when charity extends a willing hand to the hungry—when the quarrels aud ignoble passions of the swiftly-passing year are obscured and obliterated by the grasp of friendship and forgiveness—and when the lowering cloud of care upon the sorrowing man's brow dissolves in the bursting sunshine of surrounding happiness.

It was on the morning of this day, some few

years ago, I found myself walking up one of the principal streets of the Scottish capital—a stranger, in a strange place,—no very enviable position on such an occasion. I was thinking—as where is the Englishman would not?—of the last Christmas-day; and then the last Christmas-day brought to life visions of many others, till in imagination the allegorical Old Gentleman of the story-books started into life, and taking my arm with all the warmth of an old friend, together we resolved to pass the day in talking over "Auld lang syne," fully satisfied that although my years had but little then exceeded the age of boyhood, yet in the experience those years had brought we should find ample matter for reflection—ample cause for smiles, and alas, for not a few tears. From my reverie and ideal companionship I was aroused by a smart blow on the shoulder, and turning round, I beheld the familiar face of a London acquaintance. Our greeting was cordial as it was unexpected, for not having seen him for many months I was surprised to learn he had removed from one of the great surgical schools of the metropolis to complete his professional education at the Edinburgh college.

"Well, I am truly delighted to meet with you," said my friend Williams—"do you know, I was just wishing for some one to keep me company today, for I am a freshman here, and have made but few acquaintances. You are not engaged, I hope?"

"Quite the contrary—I place my time at your disposal with much pleasure, and if you were in want of a companion, I was in much the same predicament, so we may consider the meeting extremely well-timed."

"That's delightful! Then we'll have a gloriously quiet day together. I'll tell you a strong reason I have to rejoice at this chance rencontre: I have got a famous goose and plum-pudding for dinner, and we never enjoy such good things half as much by ourselves. Are they in your style at all?"

"My dear fellow, you could not hit my style better."

"I am glad of it. I have given my landlady—who by-the-bye is an obstinate but good-meaning old soul—particular directions about the goose; and as for the pudding, I sent up to London for the receipt, got the ingredients myself, mixed them in proper proportions, so that there could be no mistake, and all she has to do is to place them in a cloth and boil them. I flatter myself a first-rate affair it will be—by Jove! it makes my mouth water to think of it."

"You don't mean to say you took all this trouble for yourself?"

"No, not exactly; as it turns out, I have met

with you to join me, and I came on the look-out for some one."

"Much as I admire the taste of it," I replied, "the pudding would have waited a long time before I should have taken such precautions, I fear."

"There is nothing like being careful, my boy—especially with these Scotch Hottentots, if you have a good article, and do not wish it spoilt; besides, Christmas-day would not be Christmas-day to me, without it. Were I on my death-bed, one hundred years hence, I should imagine myself a Christmas-day short in my reckoning without such a necessary appendage to my annual enjoyments; but come along, it is getting nearly two o'clock, we must not be behind, for I have timed the boiling of it to a minute."

Away we started on our very agreeable errand. Although certainly rejoicing at the anticipation of the feast, I had still enough discretion to remember the injunction published in Poor Robin's Almanack in September, 1695:—

"Geese now in their prime season are,
Which, if well roasted, are good fare;
Yet, however, friends take heed
How too much on them you feed;
Lest, when your tongues run loose,
Your discourse do smell of goose."

Indeed, I am an epicure in good living. I hate the unwholesome olio of a foreign table-d'hote, or the gout-engendering stuffing of an aldermanic feast. Mr. Disraeli, in his admirable work, "Curiosites of Literature," tells us of a celebrated cook of the ancients, who immortalised himself by being dexterous enough to serve up a whole pig, roasted on one side and boiled on the other, whilst its inside was filled with a concoction of thrushes and other birds, slices of the matrices of a sow, the yoke of eggs, the bellies of hens with their soft eggs—the whole flavoured with a rich juice and minced-meats highly spiced. I fancy I see some "greasy, fat citizen" licking his lips at the contemplation of such an outrageous dish. Should he feel inclined to gratify his gourmandizing propensities by attempting such a *chef-d'œuvre* of the culinary art, I must refer him to the work before-named, where he will find the receipt handed down from generation to generation from the illustrious original. As a fool for his pains, I regard Apicius of old, who, residing at Minturna—a town in Vampania—took a voyage to Africa, because he heard shrimps were of a finer quality there than at the place of his sojourn, and rightly was he served when it turned out what is known in slang parlance as "a sell."

What a selfish and unpardonable glutton, too, was Philoxemus, who wished for a crane's neck, that he might be longer in swallowing his dainties, and who, when in the bath, habituated himself to swallow scalding water in order to secure the tit-bits at table, whilst the dishes were smoking hot, and others dared not attempt to touch them or their contents. The only cook I ever really had some esteem for was poor Soyer, who was possessed of a warm heart towards his fellow creatures, and did much for the poor, both soldiers and civilians, in teaching them how to make a savoury dinner off the produce of twopence.

Notwithstanding all this, I certainly do sympathise with the man whose eyes will beam joyously at the sight of a gloriously substantial piece of roast beef, reeking in its ruddy strength, filling the air with its savoury incense, so tantalizing to a hungry stomach : just so can I agree with a man who likes roast goose and plum pudding ; and it was with great pleasure I mounted to what the Scotch call "a flat"—and what we should term "the chambers"—occupied by my friend.

"Good morning, Mrs. M'Cairn," said Williams addressing the landlady, a tall, brawny Scotch-woman, who happened to be laying the cloth as we entered, "a happy Christmas to you."

"The same to you, sir, an' many o' them," was her reply. "Ye ken, sir, Lizzie's a braw wench, an' a gude wench, but she hae na been used to wait on gentlefolk, so, as it is Christmas day, I thoucht I'd gie her a wee bit help like."

"And very considerate of you; but how about the pudding?"

"Wi' muckle pains I've ta'en with it—an' I ken it'll mak' your hair curl richt weel—for it's a lang day sin ye tasted ane so gude."

"Did you hear that?" said Williams, turning to me; "you see what she thinks of it. Well, that is saying a good deal, Mrs. M'Cairn."

"I speak my mind—an' it's the gentlefolk ye bring to dinner?"

"Yes, my friend here is going to dine with me."

"Then, ye'll want twa plates, an' twa knives—an'—an'—here, Lizzy, wench—where are ye ganging the noo? It's after her I mun be looking, or she'll be fishing the plums out o' the puddin' and drowning hersel' in the pot," and away the old woman started after her small maid.

"What the devil did the old crone mean," said Williams, "by fishing out the plums and drowning herself in the pot—it can't be the pudding pot she means?"

"No," I suggested, "It's only her way of talking; unless she means the girl would try and untie the pudding cloth first, and in doing so might tumble in."

"You have hit it—that is what she meant. By Jove, it made me start, though; but, as the clown says, 'here we are,'—take your seat."

As he thus spoke in walked Mrs. M'Cairn and her miniature helpmate carrying the doomed bird, plates, condiments, &c.

"There, sir, an' a fine guse it is," said the good woman, with satisfaction, depositing it on the table.

"I perfectly agree with you; it is a beautiful bird, Mrs. M'Cairn. Look sharp with the potatoes," exclaimed Williams, rubbing his hands with uncommon delight.

"The potatoes—you have got them the noo."

"The deuce I have? It must be in my pockets, for hang me if I see them."

"I ken ye will, though, if ye cut open the guse; they're all in it's belly."

"They are all where?"

"In the guse's belly."

"The devil they are!"

"And canna you speak without bringing the de'il in. It's no richt and proper—to cook the potatoes in the guse is muckle the best way. My poor auld mon said so; an' the Lord save us, he was a judge, for he'd eat a guse to his own cheek without unbuttoning his waistcoat, he was so fond of it. Poor mon, he's dead an' gone noo! an' it's little guse he gets, I ken, where he's gone to."

"Confound it, Mrs. M'Cairn!" said Williams, "and is my taste to be measured by your old man's—so particular as I was in my directions? It is most provoking. Where is the cauliflower?"

"That is in the guse's belly, too. I boiled it a wee bit first, ye ken, then beat the potatoes and the cauliflower together, then mixed them with a wee bit o' porridge—an' the Queen hersel' oucht to rejoice at sic a dish. Come along, Lizzy, wench, for it's bad manners to talk when the gentlefolks are eating"—and away the two departed, leaving my friend and myself dumbfoundered at her volubility and her cookery.

"Well," said he at length, "did you ever hear of such a wooden-headed old stupid? The goose is spoilt—literally spoilt."

"Never mind," I replied, in a soothing tone, "it is not poison, we must make the best of it; we will revenge ourselves on the pudding."

"So we will. There is a bit of breast—by St. Patrick, what an awful mess this looks, that woman and her porridge will be the death of me. If I complain of a cold—'Nothing like porridge.' Head-ache —'Porridge for ever!' Stomach-ache—'Porridge is the stuff,' Holloway's pills are fools to it; you see she even thrusts it into my goose."

We did the best we could. Of course the goose was rendered anything but nice by Mrs. M'Cairn's new mode of cooking. A little went a long way, and a sudden pull at the bell announced our readiness for the pudding. Scarcely had the sound subsided, ere a large soup tureen made its appearance in at the door, the upper part of the body supporting it scarcely visible, and following in the tureen-bearer's wake came the miniature maid with soup plates.

"Why, what in the name of conscience have you got there?" asked Williams, staring in mute horror at the apparition, when a voice from behind the tureen replied—"Ye shall see the noo."—Upon which the earthen vessel was deposited on the table, and Mrs. M'Cairn, with a face glowing with satisfaction and red with exertion, appeared before our wondering eyes and removed the cover.

"There!" she exclaimed, with the air of a conqueror, "ken ye the like o' that before?"

"Why, what is it?" we both asked in the same breath, gazing with disgust at a nasty thick floating mess, bearing a strong resemblance to hog's wash.

"What is it?" repeated Mrs. M'Cairn—"it's the pudding—what should it be?"

"The pudding! Why, confound it, woman, it is soup!" shouted Williams.

"The Lord forgive ye for swearing—ye made it yoursel!"

"But I didn't boil it. Did you put it in a cloth?"

"Who ever hee'rd o' sic a thing—a cloth! noo—whoever boiled porridge in a cloth?—an' it's the same thing."

"Mrs. M'Cairn," said Williams, "I have before had occasion to curse your porridge—remove this horrid mess,"

"Mess! Why you mixed the ingredients yoursel; I only added a wee bit o' oatmeal to mak it sit on your stomach."

"Sit on the devil, Mrs. M'Cairn!"

"I should be very sorry to, an' it's no the act of gentlefolk to propose any sic position for a respectable female. It's unco' sorry I am to have taken half the trouble with you or your pudding either; and then to insult a puir lone body—it's awful to think aboot. Come, Lizzy, wench, an' leave the ne'er-do-weels to sit on the de'il themselves."

The indignation of the poor woman, her queer-looking head-gear, her elevated hands, and broad Scotch dialect, which I am but poorly able to illustrate, together with the indignant, wrathful, helpless expression of Williams's face, was too much for my risible faculties, and I burst into an uncontrollable fit of laughter as Mrs. M'Cairn made her exit. My friend, who was naturally a good-tempered fellow, joined me when fully sensible of the absurdity of our position, and the unpremeditated "sell," to repeat a common phrase, we had met with. Falling back on some Stilton cheese and salad, and a tolerable dessert, we endeavoured to forget our disappointment in good-tempered raillery, and so bury the shortcomings of our Christmas dinner in Scotland.

THE DEATH PHANTOMS.

"Another world encompasses us—the immaterial. That world is peopled by myriads of spirits. For what constraining cause; and when; and if ever the evil which intervenes between us and the realms of spirits is raised, and its denizens become subject to the scan of mortal eye, is a mystery about which many master-minds have reasoned, but all have failed to fathom."
BISHOP PATRICK.

"To these particulars innumerable examples might be added, all attested by grave and credible authors. But in despite of evidence which neither Bacon, Boyle, nor Johnson was able to resist, the Taish, with all its visionary properties, seems to be now universally abandoned to the use of poetry."
SIR WALTER SCOTT.

"All argument is opposed to a belief in apparitions. All experience is in its favour."
DR. JOHNSON.

IN the southern, or as it is termed by the inhabitants, the "back" part of the Isle of Wight, the scenery presents greater diversity, considering its limited extent, than perhaps any portion of the coast of England, that diversity mainly resting in its bold and undulating outline—its wild and frowning rocks and chasms. In one place we find a terrific rent, with dark, shelving rocks; in another tremendous cliffs, with huge angles four or five hundred feet high; and again, a picturesque landslip, which is but the foreground to green and verdant mountain slopes, or yellow corn fields.

To account for the widely-spread and enormously massive blocks of stone which are found in the landslips has often puzzled me, and the only conviction I ever arrived at was this: that the winter blasts, ravages of the sea, and at some very distant period, volcanic eruptions, have during the progress of ages rent and detached large tufts of earth or masses of rock from the heights on to the strand beneath: these, becoming immoveable, have gathered from the undulations of the waves, small shells, fossils and pieces of flint, until hardened by time and the petrifying quality of the water, they have at length presented their present aspect.*

---

* To those interested in the early history of this beautiful island, the following facts may not be uninteresting. They were copied by me from a work but little known, published a hundred years ago:—

"The Isle of Wight was a part of the territories anciently inhabited by the Belgæ, and was brought under subjection to the Romans during the reign of the Emperor Claudian. By them it was called Vecta, or Vectis. It was afterwards conquered by Cerdic, King of the West Saxons, who peopled it with Jutes, a tribe that had accompanied the Saxons into England. Cadwallader, a succeeding King of the West Saxons, is said to have made himself master of the same, some time after, and to have massacred most of the inhabitants.

"Having undergone many other revolutions and invasions,

To one of the deep, romantic passes of this coast, you, gentle reader, must bear me company. Supposing ourselves to have swept away the wide intervening gulf of forty years, there then stood a lonely fisherman's cottage, with rudely-built stone walls, over which the honeysuckle and clematis crept, mingling with the ivy which stretched over the mossy thatch of its roof. Before the door, a small and neat-looking garden bespoke the careful hand which cherished the little English flowers now blushing into life with the early breath of spring. Enclosing this small plot of ground stood a railed fence, with a gate opening on the narrow uneven road; a carefully gravélled little path formed the connection between the cottage and the highway, whilst the borders of this path glittered in the sunshine, with the profusion of oyster shells which in the humble taste of the owner formed its choice adornment. All this, though not bespeaking wealth, seemed to whisper of something more to be envied than that all-potent charm of life. It told of happiness, contentment, love; for none but a loving and peaceful

---

it at length, together with the islands of Jersey and Guernsey, was erected into a kingdom by King Henry VI., and bestowed on Henry de Beauchamp, Duke of Warwick, whom he crowned with his own hands; but the Duke dying without issue, these isl ands lost their royalty, and again reverted to the crown."

heart could thus have guided the willing and tasteful hand.

One evening in the month of May, after a day more than usually close and sultry, two girls advanced from the cottage and turned their steps towards the beach. They were cousins. The eldest, Jane, was a fine, healthy, well-formed lass, of about 19, with dark hair, bright, playful eyes, and a rosy, enticing mouth. The youngest seemed of more delicate figure, with fair long ringlets, blue loving eyes, and a pale, pure complexion.

"And must you, really, go home next week?" asked Mary of her cousin, looking at her with affection.

"I must, indeed, dear Mary," replied the eldest, "mother and father will be angry as it is at my having stayed so long away."

"Well, but father will tell them we cannot spare you yet."

"That would be useless—for you know poor mother is not very well, and my father can't nurse the children, and make the bread, wash the clothes, and do—I don't know how many things besides."

"I shall be so lonely when you are gone, Jane, we have had such a happy time of it these last two weeks."

"No, Mary dear, you won't be lonely, for you

are so used to be by yourself—and see what a companion you have in your garden; besides, before long, I'll get that wicked brother of yours to bring you over and see us all, and I know you will like that."

"Yes, I should, indeed; so will he—for although you call him wicked you know very well how much you love him, and I am very sure he loves you, for he thinks of nobody else: it is 'Jane's this,' and 'Jane's the other,' till I declare I am getting quite jealous."

"Hush, Mary, that is too bad; he might be listening behind some of the rocks or bushes, and then how stupid I should look—though, to speak the truth, do you wonder at my liking him? You know what a good kind brother and son he has always been."

"To be sure, I do; it is that which makes me jealous, to think of losing him. Why, father often says we should have starved during that long illness of his if it had not been for Bob. He worked night and day then, and has thought of no one else but us since my poor mother's death until you seemed to run in his head; but, never mind, my dear father will be left me, and no one except death can take him away."

"No, but you will be taking yourself away one of these days, Mary."

"Taking myself away! What do you mean?

"What should I mean, but marrying."

"No, Jane—no, never! Upon my mother's deathbed I promised to be to my dear rough old father all that a child should be, when he has no one else to comfort or understand him; and whilst he lives I want no stranger to love. I know my own heart, but I cannot read another's: those who might love me would never love my father."

"We shall see, Miss Dutiful—we shall see." By this time they had arrived on the beach, where two men were preparing their nets and casting them into their boat, which lay high and dry upon the strand.

"Well, Jane, lass!" said a tall muscular man, with browned and deeply-wrinkled visage and iron-gray hair, which floated in rude locks beneath his broad sou'wester, "have thee come to give us a haul?"

"Yes, uncle, to be sure we have; and Mary here will lend a hand, too."

"Mary!" said the old man, as his eyes beamed with affection when they looked upon his darling, "Mary, indeed! Why, she ain't got the strength of a spider. Thee art the lass; leastways Bob here says there be none like thee."

"Now, then, father, what a jolly blab you are," cried a tall, healthy, fine-looking young fellow at the old man's side—bearing too strong a resemblance for their relationship to be mistaken—"Don't believe him, Jane." As the hardy young fisherman said this, the warm blood which mounted into his open, manly face convinced the observant and laughing girls the old man had spoken the truth.

"Look, father!" said Mary, clapping her hands, "Robert is blushing; well, I declare, who would have thought his face could ever be a deeper red than it always is."

"Only wait 'till I get the chance," said Robert, hiding his confusion by busying himself with the nets, "I'll pay thee out for this, lass, I warrant me."

"Now, my lad, let's heave her adrift."

"Ay, ay, father," answered Robert, glad of escaping from the other subject, and at the same time getting a peculiar contrivance, which fishermen have for floating their boats."

"Here, we'll both help: come along, Mary, you push on that side, and I'll push on this," said Jane, planting herself beside the young fisherman.

"Get away with thee—thee girl, thou be'est always in the way when thee'rt not wanted." What sad hypocrites we sometimes are when our affections are concerned! The old man was so when he said this, judging by the tender smile which lighted up his rough face.

"Don't say that, father; you know you would break your dear old heart without me," said Mary.

"Now, lad, a long pull and a strong pull—heave with a will."

"And altogether," cried Jane, taking up the old man's tone, as she pushed at the bulky craft, and made the cliffs echo with her noisy mirth.

"Once more, dad," said Robert. As he said this he took advantage of the close proximity of Jane's face to imprint on it a hearty kiss.

"Avast, there!" cried the old man; "so that be the fish thee'rt catching, Bob—do you call that lending a hand?"

"No," said the girl, "it is lending me a kiss to be repaid with a box on the ears"; and away the two started, chasing each other like children, heedless of the would-be cross old father, who when he found out the impossibility of his working himself into a passion, leant against the boat, and fairly roared with laughter at the gambols of the two girls and his son. At length Robert returned: the girls were following, but the old man turned them back, knowing too well the boat would never float with such assistants. Left to themselves they soon launched her, and with a few strokes of the oar she careered over the long-swelling waves just as the setting sun disappeared down the western hemisphere. The boat passed out of sight, and the two girls slowly wended their way to the cottage. With approaching darkness came that strange, dull, almost unearthly stillness so beautifully described by Thomson :—

"A boding silence reigns
Dread through the dull expanse; save the dull sound
That from the mountain, previous to the storm,
Rolls o'er the muttering earth, disturbs the flood,
And shakes the forest leaf without a breath.
Prone to the lowest vale, ærial tribes
Descend, the tempest-loving raven scarce
Dares wing the dubious dusk. In rueful gaze
The cattle stand, and on the scowling heavens
Cast a deploring eye, by man forsook,
Who to the crowded cottage hies him fast,
Or seeks the shelter of the downward cave."

The two cousins sat at the open casement and quietly chatted as they watched the falling shadows.

"Mary, you are right, it is very lonely in a cottage like this, amongst the rocks, so far away from any other; I wonder how you can bear it, when your father and brother are sometimes away so many hours!"

"Do you know, Jane, at times I think I have learnt to like it. I sit at this window, or in my little garden outside, and work; and when I am tired of work, I sit and think."

"Yes; but what is the use of thinking, if you have not any one to tell your thoughts to? Why I should almost lose the use of my tongue. But pray, what do you think about ?"

"I scarcely know; sometimes of my mother, sometimes of my father or brother, wondering if they will ever be parted from me. Then I think of how many fish they will catch, or a thousand other things."

"Jane !' said Mary, suddenly changing her tone, "I feel so strange to-night—so—so—well, I don't know how, exactly."

"That is all through some idle fancy you have got, I'll be bound !"

"Perhaps it is; but I am certain something dreadful is going to happen."

"What nonsense, my dear; just because the sky looks dark, and the air is so still. Tell me, Mary, do you never really think of marriage ?"

"No; very seldom at least. I dare say it is very well in its way."

"Only think of the pleasure, now, of being one's own mistress !"

"Yes; but that luxury is sometimes purchased by many hardships. I feel almost suffocated with the heat !" And throwing the lattice still wider open, she looked towards the sea. "Jane, look ! the clouds are so dark, and do you hear the waves rolling upon the beach, and dashing against the rocks ? How quickly the sea has risen !"

"I thought we were going to have a storm, the air has been so close all day."

"God preserve my father and brother," murmured Mary, heedless of her cousin's remark. "I never felt so sadly as I do to-night."

"Come, you must not be timid, you are a fisherman's daughter; although we feel dull, it is only in the air."

"No, no, it is more than that." As Mary spoke thus she withdrew herself from the casement, and sank into a chair. Her face had turned deadly white, whilst tears, like drops of dew, slowly fell down her cheeks.

"Why, Mary, dear, you look so frightened! let me close the shutters."

"No, not yet, not yet."—At that moment a vivid flash of lightning shot like a fiery arrow through the sky, and the thunder broke as a fierce cannonade upon the unnatural stillness of the air.

"Close the shutters, and shut out the storm," cried Mary, hiding her face in her hands.

"No, no, you selfish little thing; you said no, and now I say no; it is not often one gets the chance of seeing a storm like this, so close to the sea. Come, let me put my arm round your waist, and we'll watch it together. Hark at the rain! it is falling in torrents: poor uncle and Robert, they will be drenched,"

"If that is the only ill that befalls them I shall not care. Oh, how dreadful!" This exclamation was occasioned by another intensely vivid flash of lightning which lit up the sea, the heavens, and surrounding rocks in one brilliant glare, whilst a strong sulphuric almost choking vapour filled the atmosphere.

"Oh, beautiful! how beautiful!" cried Jane, clapping her hands together, her dark eyes, in their excitement, gleaming like stars, as she viewed the marvellous grandeur of the tempest; but she was recalled to herself by hearing her cousin's voice exclaiming—

"Oh, come away! Oh, pray, come away! I cannot bear it."

Unable to penetrate that strange presaging cloud which, in the hour of coming evil, will so often, like a dark shadow, step within our path and lay its icy hand upon the quick pulsation of our hearts, Jane looked upon the poor timid girl, who sat crouching in a distant corner of the cottage, with an eye of wondering pity, and then with soothing words approached and knelt down at her side.

"Don't leave me, Jane; let us stay here until the storm is over: it is time to go to bed, but I would not go there for the world now. I think I should have died to-night if you had not been with me."

"Why, you silly one, you have not half the courage I have. What time is it, I wonder? There is another flash—how vivid! I'll shut the window, dear!"

"No, no!—never mind: I can't let you leave me now," said Mary, drawing herself still closer to Jane, and laying her head upon her breast, whilst her long bright locks flowing loosely down occasionally became radiant in the electric flash. The only sounds which broke upon the loneliness were the raging of the storm without and the gentle soothing of the brave girl, who sat immoveable with her eyes fixed upon the open casement; so they watched the black and starless firmament, whilst Jane's hands unconsciously played with the golden locks of her cousin. Thus they remained until the hour of midnight, when the wind having risen, the shutters, which had broken from their fastenings, lapped to and fro upon the rusty hinges threatening the demolition of the glass at every stroke.

"Mary, I must go out and close the shutters now, or the windows will be broken—don't be afraid, I shall not be a minute," said Jane, encouragingly, pressing the other's hand, and speaking in whispers, as if afraid of rousing the spirit of the storm: even her strong heart had gradually yielded to the utter loneliness of her situation. The other poor girl did not answer; but mechanically releasing her from her grasp, sat motionless as Jane went to the door, and opening it looked out.

The rain had ceased, and the wind came with fitful moaning gusts up the chine, bearing on its saline breath the noisy throbbings of the broad channel waters. Just peering above the vapour of a wild, black mass of clouds, the moon was mistily shining—not a star was visible—and as the young girl gazed out upon the darkness, a thrill of terror for a single moment ran through her veins. But hers was not the spirit to be easily daunted. Recovering herself, with a firm step she passed out into the little garden, and as she closed the shutters she could just perceive the white form of her cousin, who had slightly altered her position, so that her face was turned towards a small window in the back part of the cottage, which, nearly abutting upon the rocks that rose perpendicularly above, left but little room for the reflexion of the storm. Jane had closed the shutters, and was turning to approach the door, when immediately outside the little gate she beheld a strange and unearthly phantom. Its form resembled that of a man, though much taller. It was white—transparent—cloud-like; the left arm was extended towards the sea, and the features, if such they could be called, seemed those of her cousin Robert in death. With the immediate evil in view came that natural strength of mind which God has implanted in the hearts of so many of the softer sex, to make our lordly natures blush. With firm, unfaltering steps Jane advanced towards the shadow. It did not recede. At that moment, when she was within a few feet of it, a shriek loud and shrill came from the cottage, and made the rocky caverns and recesses echo again and again. With the shriek the phantom vanished; and Jane rushed back to her cousin, whom she found outstretched, and apparently lifeless upon the floor.

Her first thought was to get a light. After searching for some time, she discovered a few matches; but in her eagerness they would not ignite. She came to the last,—it sputtered, threw out a blue phosphoric gleam, and went out. Can words paint her situation? Her cousin struck down by some unknown terror—her own heart, in its reaction, almost palsied by the strange shadow but just seen, and the long hours of solitude and darkness. For a time she sat and bathed with water the forehead of her cousin, who, at length reviving, and finding in whose arms she lay, clung to her with all the fear and dependence of a child when on its mother's bosom.

"Come, come, my dear," said Jane, "what has made you so frightened?"

"Don't leave me again!" murmured the poor girl. "The shadow at the window—so very dreadful!"

"What shadow?" asked her cousin, stifling her agitation.

"My father!—my poor father!—I saw him there at that window. He is dead—heaven help me! I know he is, for his spirit pointed to the sea," and at the same time she stretched her hand towards the little window abutting upon the rocks at the back of the room.

"You have been dreaming, Mary!" faltered out Jane.

"No, no, it was not a dream; for I saw it so distinctly through the darkness, and I thought I heard a cry, like that of drowning men. My poor father and brother! Oh bring them back to me again!—oh bring them back!"

Jane, with a heart foreboding a great sorrow, tried to comfort and calm the fears of her cousin, and at length proposed that they should go upstairs to bed.

"No, no," responded Mary, "it would be useless; I cannot sleep."

"But we can pray," replied Jane. "Come, Mary, there is no sorrow so great, we may not seek comfort and find it with the Almighty let us go upstairs together, and He is sure to listen to our prayers if we place our trust in Him."

Clinging to each other, the two girls went upstairs into their small bedroom, and falling on their knees, long and earnestly they prayed for the preservation of those dear ones they had left but a few hours previously, rich in manhood, health and happiness. Without undressing, they at length sought their bed, and locked in each other's embrace waited for the morning's dawn. At length it broke, cloudless and beautiful: the very air teemed with freshness, the singing of the birds, and the odour of wild flowers; not one vestige remained of all the havoc and terror of the night, but a few torn branches, the damp earth, and swollen water-courses.

Mary, exhausted, had sunk into a feverish slumber, whilst Jane, pale and anxious, stood by her side watching and listening for the sound of approaching footsteps up from the beach. They came at length, and with eager joy and thankfulness she ran down stairs and opened the cottage door. At the little gate she beheld, not the well-known faces of her betrothed and his father, but that of an old fisherman, whose dim eyes were suffused with tears, and whose kind, rough heart caused his words to falter and his tongue to refuse its office as he told the sad tale. The boat of the fisherman had been dashed to pieces on the rocks, and both father and son had perished. The time, midnight—the hour of the Phantoms ! !

NOTE.—I have quoted several opinions at the commencement of this sketch which are entitled to great respect, as coming from men so celebrated, and proving as they do the great doubt that exists with respect to a supernatural spirit world. Like many others, I endeavour to disbelieve what to us mortals is so utterly void of comprehension; and yet, as in the above tale, we meet with startling occurrences, sworn to by eye-witnesses whom we have no reason or right to doubt.

It was very many years after the events here recorded, circumstances brought me in contact with the Jane of my sketch, and to her I am indebted for a graphic and minute description of the particulars. She was, at the time I met with her, a respectable and respected widow lady, with two daughters. On my expressing some degree of doubt as to the reality of the phantoms, except in her own and her cousin's imaginations, labouring as they were under great fear and excitement, her reply was somewhat as follows:—"Sir, it is many years ago: I was then a girl, I am now an old woman; yet even now, at times, I recall that shadow as vividly as it then stood before me. I have no reason or motive for telling you an untruth; and besides, if I had been deceived, how was it my cousin was struck down with terror at the same time by an exactly similar shadow? She, poor girl, never recovered the fright and the sorrow which it so truly foreboded, but gradually withered, as it were, into her grave. I am not superstitious, and know how difficult such things are to believe, but to the day of my death I cannot forego the evidence of my own eyes." This certainly was a strong argument—let the reader contend with it to his satisfaction.

WIGGENS IN SEARCH OF LODGINGS:

A NEW CHRISTMAS STORY,

BEING A "TRUE ACCOUNT" OF THE EXPERIENCES OF MR. AND MRS. WIGGENS DURING THE SHORT SPACE OF ONE FORTNIGHT WHILST LODGING-HUNTING IN MANCHESTER.

"Who is't can say, I am at the worst?
I am worse than e'er I was."

SHAKESPEARE.

In discarding the newly-adopted method of romance writers when addressing the imagination of their readers for the first time, as thus:—"On one fine morning in the month of June, a solitary traveller might be seen wending his way," &c. &c., we adopt the good old hackneyed phraseology of "once upon a time;" so to commence:—

Once upon a time, in the township of Hulme, one of the suburbs of the great manufacturing emporium of Manchester, there resided two lovely young virgins, rejoicing in the very apropos cognomen of "Lily,"; they were born of respectable parents, their mother being the daughter of an innkeeper in a small country town, the fact of which proves the possibility or the impossibility of that lady's observation, "she had all her life been used to the best society." Nor, perhaps, was it less true, "I was born to ride in my father's carriage," he having been possessed of an antediluvian four-wheel, constructed shortly after the year one, in which the ex-carriage, ex-cab, ex-cart, and now job-horse, occasionally did duty when not otherwise employed, and his wind permitted. On arriving at a marriageable age, the mother of the Lilies united herself to a gentleman of equal position in life, and in the course of time and nature gave to the arms of the doting father the two virgins beforenamed: he dying, left his widow his property, consisting of his great-grandfather's six teaspoons, one mustard, two dessert, and the top of a pepper-box, comprising the family plate.

The lady, unwilling to "waste her sweetness on the desert air," was united a second time, to a gentlemanly follower of Crispin, in other words, "a cobbler," who had the weaknesses natural to that intellectual and obliging class, viz.—a sportive love of gambling, drinking, and never working on the Monday, by which means he greatly reduced the estate possessed by his wife in right of her father, producing the handsome annual income of about forty pounds, being the entire rental of no less than fourteen handsome dwellings. The daughters deeming themselves disgraced by the alliance, at once retired, taking with them the *family plate*; and having acquired by their own industry sufficient means to make a start in life, took up their residence in a mansion unembellished by the Italian, Roman, Elizabethian, or early English style of architecture, but suiting more their virgin tastes and the trite apothegm of "beauty unadorned is then adorned the most." It was furnished with equal simplicity, and quiet unobtrusive elegance; and whilst passing away their time in some ladylike yet profitable employment, they sweetly caroll'd the live-long day, (except when they quarrelled, which was very often), and the passer-on would pause at the sound of their voices, doubtful whether he listened to the nightingale or the more plaintive cry of the owl. Sometimes they would vary the monotony by the youngest discoursing most eloquent music on a concertina with a cold, that she happened to be in the rudiments of instruction with; or by the eldest *executing* "Rule Britannia" with variations, on a comb.

Near their abode lived a gentleman, by the name of Wiggens, a quiet man, attached to the order of Melpomone, and his charming, amiable, and accomplished young wife. I dare not attempt to describe her, but at once refer you to the beauties of James's novels, in his best style, where pages are employed to pourtray such pictures in words, where roses, lilies, pearls, diamonds, alabaster—all hide their diminished heads, and are disconcerted by the lady's cheeks, teeth, eyes, nose, mouth, &c.; and as such perfections of loveliness are so frequently to be met with in this busy life amongst our sisters of clay, we must of conscience believe the said portraits to be natural. Suffice it to say, that Mrs. Wiggens was supposed to surpass them all—in her hair especially, which was only equalled by a heroine of domestic romance lately seriously described in one of our weekly journals of murder, love, and suicide, which ran as follows:—"Her hair flowed in graceful curls to the ground, and then TURNED UP AGAIN!—it was black as the raven's wing, &c." But enough of this. Wiggens, having determined to change his residence, and observing a card inviting inspection in the window of the Lilies, therein entered, and struck by the form, features, and intellectual bearing of the fullest blown Lily—whose incessant grin possessed an indescribable charm, awakening the most lively and exciting astonishment, that—from the great extent of the cavity—a division had not long since taken place, he at once came to terms, and thus shared their roof, and with his wife formed an interesting addition to this amiable family.

Some few months had passed over, when Wiggens—thoughtless man!—introduced a most unwelcome visitor in the shape of a dog. Poor fellow, he had long wanted a dog, and on being offered one by a friend at once accepted it. Little thought he of the storm about to burst over his domestic felicity: he saw not the frowns of his lovely wife, he heard not her happy, joyous, and ever-contented voice grow deep and threatening—he saw only his dog, he heard only its merry bark, he watched only its wagging tail, and he brought it home. Then the peace of his hearth was shattered at a blow—an earthquake shook the visionary fabric on which he had built long and delightful walks, through the green meadows, with his canine companion. The Lily (I mean the full-blown one) became indignant at the animal's dirty feet—even the door mat was denied him for repose. The Lily fastened up her window curtains, she threw off the nature of "the lamb," and assumed "the lion," administering kicks to the poor dog every opportunity, until Wiggens' ire rose with the occasion—he grew determined. The female Wiggens, previously incensed against the damsels for adopting a method highly to be recommended to all dishonest landladies, who have a desire to put a damper on your fire—viz., to well water your coals before putting them on—that is to say, if they are included in the rent—and this good lady observing, from the majestic deportment of her loved lord, "he was fixed as fate," at once gave notice. Despite the elements being unpropitious—despite of snow, rain, and cold—Wiggens and his dog departed on the difficult task of discovering a new abode, and thus laid the foundation for the forthcoming adventures and this new Christmas story, it being close upon that period. Apartments at length he obtained, and when the shades of evening had fallen on the busy streets, and the gas-lamps gleamed with a bilious lustre through the foggy and smoky atmosphere, Wiggens removed his traps, and with his traps his wife and dog. As the clock of a neighbouring church announced to all who were in the way to hear it the hour of eleven, they were once more seated by the domestic hearth, looking round upon their handsomely-furnished abode with complacent eyes, and snugly ensconcing themselves in rosewood-framed easy chairs, whilst the dog squatted on his haunches between them, winked at the fire, and ever and anon wagged his tail, and looking up into their faces, seemed to remark with all the satisfaction of the clown in the pantomime, "Here we are!" To complete their felicity, the spirit of beer whispered in the ear of Wiggens, a little would be enjoyable; the beverage is therefore ordered and procured—though not without trepidation was the command given, as a tall, fine-looking woman, in a black silk dress, was likely to have a soul above the fetching and carrying of malt. In this instance it was not so—the beer was brought; but, alas! did the Wiggenses dream? Was it a jug? or the shadow of a very nasty, big, yellow-looking, vulgar jug that appeared? Could people possessed of such furniture serve their genteel lodgers with such offensive-looking earthenware? The dream was at once dispelled by the landlady knocking at the door—"she wanted the jug"—it was the only one they possessed, and the spirit of her husband, like that of Wiggens, yearned for beer. With a light heart, jug in hand, the landlord departed, when, not being firm upon his pins, and the door steps being frozen over, a crash was heard—he has fallen, smashed the solitary jug, and unable to get another, retires chopfallen and beerless to bed, whilst visions of future malt fade before the soul of Wiggens, as the crash of the earthenware gave the last notes of its departure. Some people have accommodating dispositions; such had the Wiggenses on this occasion. Retiring to bed, and finding it minus sheets, after having first held a philosophical discussion on the wholesomeness of blankets they nestled themselves in the same, and sank into the arms of Morpheus.

The morning having long since dawned, it being

in fact, past nine o'clock, the male Wiggens awoke from out a feverish sleep, when lo! upon the air a wailing cry arose which thrilled through every nerve. 'Twas not a human creature—no; 'twas a dog. Wiggens knew the voice—'twas his dog! His elbow immediately came in contact with female Wiggens's ribs, who being desired to "get up," did so, in the fond and foolish hope of washing and dressing; but, alas! for human wishes, and—

> "Hope! fortune's cheating lottery!
> Where for one prize a hundred blanks there be!"

The tooth-glass had lost its bottom, the jug was empty—I mean of water, not dirt, the latter article it favoured—and the towel-horse stood skeleton-like in a corner, unadorned with linen, all of which, in the utter weariness of the previous night's flitting, had been overlooked.

Female Wiggens immediately proceeded downstairs, when looking through the kitchen window, she beheld her lord's faithful animal huddled up and trembling in a corner of the yard, whence he had been ejected by the landlady, who was standing over him, about to administer a token of her admiration by way of a kick, when her leg was checked in mid-air by the vision of her new lodger's nightcap at the window. The owner of that nightcap having protected the dog so far, looked around her. The parlour fire was unlit, breakfast seemed a very distant achievement, all looked cold, tawdry, and miserable; the lady in black silk was now a sloven in cotton. Strange as it may appear, as the ire of female Wiggens increased it fell upon her spouse's dog as the author of all. With hasty strides she remounts the stairs, and with angry glances at her lord demands of him the dismissal of herself or the unfortunate animal. Male Wiggens remonstrated, but women when they make up their minds are proverbially obstinate. His pleading did not soften a wrinkle on her face; he felt he must part from one, and decided upon his canine companion. On rising, he even goes to the butcher's and countermands the liver he had ordered, which to his surprise he found had been already done by his wife, the fact of which positively encouraged the man of mutton to grin, and indulge in a joke at the expense of Wiggens, alluding in an indirect manner to his "missus" wearing the unmentionables; but the joke was profitable only to the joker. Wiggens spurned the base insinuation and gazed at his dog, who, whilst wagging his tail looked around upon the tempting bits, selecting those most agreeable to his palate, and licking his lips in imagination of the dainty morsels. With disappointment he followed his master from the shop, and showed no more a pleased alacrity, until meeting with some friendly animal who whispered in his ear doubtless the last new joke bandied about by the canine fraternity, the reflection of which set his tail again in motion, and that was the last action noted by his disconsolate master, on parting with him in a new and strange home where he had conveyed him after four days, proprietorship.

Besides the little disagreeables before spoken of, the new landlady of the Wiggenses had certain singularly original notions, that might have been very excusable in a Robinson Crusoe or an Alexander Selkirk, but appeared rather peculiar to their nicer tastes. For instance, she preferred the aid of a dust pan to cook a mutton chop with to a gridiron, believed a plate full of fat was necessary fully to enjoy it, had a great disgust for table-coverings or superfluous knives and forks, thought spoons unnecessary, and deemed one glass amply sufficient for any number. All this not suiting the somewhat fastidius taste perhaps of Wiggens, after the third meal in the house he determined upon paying a week's rent and at once departing, which determination that afternoon he most faithfully carried out, turning his back upon their late lodgings with the moral reflection, God help the "poor genteel!" who sacrifice everything for an outward show, who grub on from day to day, silk and rags! silk and rags! and more especially heaven help the man who, on a labourer's income, takes to himself "a young lady" wife, as the phrase goes, "well brought up," which generally defined, means she has learnt all the ignorance a boarding-school miss is supposed to acquire, and turns up her nose at making a pudding, cooking a chop, or properly washing her face, when there is only her husband to look at it.

So again did Wiggens remove his traps, his wife—but alas! not his dog—to a new abode, discovered under the disadvantage of a pelting shower, and a thick grimy deposit of dirt on the pavements, with a dull and sooty air, the natural consequences of a Manchester atmosphere.

Mrs. Wiggens was delighted with the exterior of her new home, as they approached in a cab. "So nice and clean—such a very quiet, respectable-looking house." It certainly was somewhat strange the amount of attention from the neighbours on their arrival; heads might be seen through Venetian blinds, behind damask curtains, and over wire blinds. Now, Wiggens was naturally a modest man, and was therefore not a little surprised at the conduct of the new landlady; her domestic being assisting upstairs with his boxes, the said lady amused herself by pushing at the fleshy protuberance on the lower portion of the girl's back, and occasionally imparting a pinch thereto, whether to aid her locomotion or give fresh zest to the merriment apparently existing between them, to Wiggens was doubtful. They say, "Familiarity breeds contempt," and following the suggestion the prospect was decidedly not cheering; but the rooms being very inviting, and a little rest positively necessary, the new lodgers resolved to make the best of it. We will pass over various little peculiarities in the consumption of tea and sugar and put it down to evaporation—we will not even transcribe the new landladlady's enforced familiarity, or her history, which had been confided to female Wiggens immediately on male Wiggens turning his back—no, suffice it, three days are gone and Sunday at length has arrived, and in the evening returning to his domicile, the said gentleman, to his surprise found a great crowd surrounding the door, and people pointing to him as an object of curiosity as he ascended the steps. On entering the house what was his horror to run plump into the arms of a policeman, to have the bull's eye of a second turned upon him, and to feel himself dragged by the neck by his wife, who was calling loudly for his protection. His amazed but dignified presence somewhat restored peace, and then did he learn—the wife had been beating the landlord, and the landlord had been beating the domestic, who, five feet ten in her stockings, had wisely flown for protection behind the young and lovely female Wiggens, who stood four feet nothing in her Balmorals. The latter lady deeming discretion the better part of valour, and the use of her lungs on such an occasion indispensable, had boldly sallied out, screaming lustily, into the street, and seizing hold of an aged, decrepid veteran of ninety, had dragged him into the fray, who, whilst the cries of "murder!" grew fast and furious, contented himself by exclaiming, "Dear, deary me! what is the matter? Is anybody a hurtin' anybody?" in a voice long since descended to "childish treble notes." The worst of calamities must have an end, so apparently had this, when the ill-fated Wiggens at once informed the lady of the house he and his wife were quiet, modest people, unused to such notoriety, and must perforce retire from the scene of action on the following Saturday. Then, foolishly dreaming the peace of all parties comparatively restored, they adjourned to bed; but, ere many minutes had elapsed, footsteps echoed through the passages—more and more furious grew the landlady's voice, who had falsely lulled the unsuspicious lodgers into seeming security—crash! went the sound of crockery—bang! went the flying furniture—the smell of fire was distinctly visible, and the Wiggenses tremble, in the sheets, picturing the house in flames and themselves wandering in search of shelter through the cold streets, with nothing but their night gear—two interesting objects. Not until morning dawned did the tempest subside, and then did they congratulate themselves their night's expectations had not been realized, for not only had the amiable tigress of the house broken the furniture and burnt the table cloths, but even the Wiggenses' dips had not been held sacred—two pounds of them had been ruthlessly cast upon the flames to increase their fury.

This was of course past endurance, and once more the male Wiggens departs on his mission for lodgings. Door after door reverberates beneath his hand—house after house he enters—street after street he wanders through. Of course it was raining, it had hardly left off for three months; useless it would be to enumerate the grubby children who would insist on wiping their hands on his trousers, or getting between his legs, crying out, "Daddy, Daddy!" at which the mothers look at Wiggens, and smirk, as much as to say, "Don't you feel proud of being taken for a father;" but with a frown he rebukes them—his heart is adamant—he feels not one throb of a daddy in his breast, for he knows that he is childless. Vain would it be to tell of the communicative old ladies who, getting the amiable Wiggens into a corner, relate to him the history of themselves and their ancestry to the earliest generation, the qualities of their lodgers, their occupations, and a few remarks upon the lodgers of their neighbours. No; let all this pass, and we will speak of one episode alone, when attracted by a more than usually respectable exterior, Wiggens at once agitated the knocker, and the following was the result:—A female appeared —a tall, stout, fresh-coloured, young and grimy individual, with a dress formed after the fashion of Joseph's garment of many colours, supported on all sides by pins.

WIGGENS:—"Can I see the landlady?"

FEMALE:—"I be the landlady."

WIGGENS (with surprise):—Are you, indeed?"

FEMALE: "Yes, I be; come in, sir. Mind, now, you were nearly in that there pail (he having stumbled over the same, in the middle of the passage.) I'm a-washin to-day."

WIGGENS: Ah, yes; the passage, nothing else I suppose?"

FEMALE: "No, I doesn't trouble soap and water too often; it ain't good."

"*Ain't it?*" said Wiggens, wondering how long it could possibly be since she had cleansed her skin, and continuing—"Well, I will not come any further. I came to look at your lodgings, but I don't think they will suit."

"Why, you ain't see'd 'em yet, young man. Oh, lawks! drat that child," said the woman, pointing to a dirty little creature in the kitchen, "if he hasn't gone and emptied the shovel of dust into the bread pan. I'll kill yer, yer young warmint." And away she darted, bringing captive back her offspring, a worthy branch from such a tree, on whose flesh a prolific crop of mustard and cress might have been cultivated, and who commenced crying with all his might. "Hold yer tongue, or else this here gent will take you away, so I tells yer—yer little devil," continued the lady.

"The Fates preserve me from such an incumbrance," thought Wiggens, at the same time the female applied the cloth she was cleaning the passage with to the pimple or apology in the shape of a nose on the face of her cherub.

"This is the blessedest young'un you ever see'd for mischief, sir; he's the the image of his father."

"What an interesting family," thought Wiggens, adding aloud, "Good day!"

"Ain't yer a going to look at my lodgings? I'll take yer in and do for yer; you'd be very comfortable, and I'm a stunner to cook."

"No doubt about it," said Wiggens. "My good woman, you would effectually do for me in a week if I entered your house; as I said before, 'Good day.'" And away he walked, followed by her abuse; that he heeded not, for he was reflecting on the errors we are continually making in this world by arriving at conclusions from a decent exterior, of the falsity of which his lodging-hunting had afforded many examples. There was another melancholy reflection — should he be compelled to wander about the streets in this unsettled condition until Christmas-day, how was Mrs. Wiggens to indulge in that custom so endeared to us at this time of year by the habits of our forefathers, and the recollections of our own earlier years, viz., "having a Christmas pudding on a Christmas-day?" Ever since the last she had dreamt and talked much of an experiment to be tried that might possibly prevent it from having the solidity of a cricket ball, as on that occasion. Wiggens knew if Mrs. W. was disappointed the blame would fall upon his innocent head, and even the memory of his dog would not remain scathless; he felt the happiness of not only his *Christmas-day*, but many days after, depended on that pudding, so with fresh energy he set to work, and at length his peregrinations ceased. He decided upon a another and seemingly comfortable abode. On again paying a week's rent in advance to the amiable tigress and ruthless destroyer of his "dips," he departed, and was last seen entering within the precincts of his new home, with the female Wiggens's jar of onions in one hand and her work-basket in the other—bearing goodwill towards all men, hoping to spend, if not a merry, at least a comfortable Christmas-day, and a happier New Year!

A STRANGE SUICIDE.

Oh! deaf to nature, and to heaven's command!
Against thyself to lift the murdering hand;
O damn'd despair! to shun the living light,
And plunge thy guilty soul in endless night!

LUCRETIUS.

On a certain night in the spring of 1852, any one passing along the main road leading from G——, a small market town in one of the southern counties, would certainly have paused to remark a beautiful little English cottage, situate to the right of the traveller, if leaving the adjacent town. It was a two-storeyed gable-roofed building of the good old style of architecture, with pretty, quaint-looking chimney pots, trelliced windows, and walls concealed with ivy, jasmine, or clematis. It had a neat wooden porch, redolent with the climbing rose and the sweet honeysuckle, a smooth green lawn, flowers of various hues in every nook and corner, the graceful fuchsia, the scented heliotrope, and the brilliant geranium. The windows fairly gleamed in the snow-like whiteness of their adornments, and from every lattice lights reflected brightly, whilst the blinds were turned into so many Fantoccini's with human figures for their shadows, and sounds of music and revelry stole upon the still night air.

The stars might be counted in myriads, so clear and beautiful was the sky, whilst the moon shone so brightly that every object was rendered distinctly visible. In the flower garden, at the back of the cottage, walked a young man of about twenty-five. His features were regular and handsome, his complexion dark, his large intelligent eyes hazel. He paced with hurried steps, sometimes abruptly pausing, but with his eyes intently fixed upon the heavens, and occasionally he might have been heard to murmur—" Strange, very strange ! Are they worlds ? Would death reveal ?" At length his attention was attracted by a figure in white advancing towards him from the house, and a light step resounding on the gravel walk. It was the form of a pretty fair-haired girl, with long shining tresses, rosy lips, and bright blue eyes.

" Come, Walter," she said, and her voice floated on the air soft as the cadence of an Æolian harp— " Papa and all our friends are wondering at your absence. What a dull boy you are, to prefer walking about here in the dark !"

" Nay, it is not dark, Kate ; look, what a lovely night. How bright the stars are !"

"I don't wish to look at them when you are near me, Walter. In your face I see the only star I care for: should that cease shining on me——"

"And what then, my bonny Kate?" he asked.

"The world to me would then be darkness. Yet I would think that from the brightest of all, your soul looked down upon me."

"God bless you, Kate! you are my own darling," he exclaimed.

"But come, Walter, come to papa; they will not remain longer without you. Papa says you are the life of the party, and so you are."

"Yes, but I am warm now, let me remain here a few minutes longer. You will, won't you my pretty bird?" As he spoke this he parted the ringlets from off her brow, and gazed into the depths of her loving eyes. "You are my own bonny Kate, are you not?" he continued; but no words issued from her lips, yet the sunny smile which suffused her features, and the warm blood mantling to her brow, gave an eloquent reply.

"Why will you not come with me?" she asked, as if to avoid his question, "do you really wish to walk here alone?"

"Well, it is such a lovely night, and the flowers smell so sweetly. You cannot think how refreshing it is to breathe the pure air, after being almost stifled in that warm room,"

"Still, Walter, you seemed to enjoy yourself. Were you not doing so?"

"Yes, Kate; but yet you must confess, in all these parties there are a great many silly people; and besides, although I am merry, you must not always think I am happy."

"Not happy!" she said, "not happy! I did not notice it before. Are you angry with me?"

"What nonsense, dearest: can I ever be angry with you?"

"I don't know; some people are angry and cannot give any particular reason for it. A thoughtless word will often unconsciously wound; therefore, although I have tried to be good, you may be angry with me." As she spoke thus, a bright tear glided down her cheek. There are few men who can see a woman weep without emotion, especially a young and pretty one: so Walter thought as he kissed her, and putting his arm round her waist, turned her tears to laughter by a well-timed joke, and together they passed into the cottage, happier than ever, bearing out the following stanza of Scott's:—

"The rose is fairest when 'tis budding new,
And hope is brightest when it dawns from fears;
The rose is sweetest washed with morning dew,
And love is loveliest when embalmed with tears."

In order to give more interest to this story, it is

necessary to put the reader on familiar terms with the persons concerned.

Kate Vincent was one of two sisters. Her father had been some two years previously in a wealthy and influential position in the neighbouring borough town; but owing to an unfortunate speculation he was considerably reduced in circumstances, and his wife dying about this time, he at once retired from a mercantile life, with the small residue of his property, and taking Ivy Cottage resolved to lead a quieter existence with his two daughters. But a man used to active business habits can seldom rest without employment of some kind: an appointment being vacant in one of the parochial offices, he applied, and from the deserved respect in which he was held, he at once obtained it. Kate was the eldest child, possessing a sweet disposition, and a pretty winning face, as already described. With such recommendations, I need hardly say, she had many suitors—or would-be—numbering about the usual aggregate of sensible men, of manly lovers, and sighing donkeys. The one selected by her father, and by the warmer dictates of her own heart, was Walter Worthington, a young man of good connections, station, and habits, whilst with the ladies he possessed, in his handsome face and most agreeable manners, still stronger recommendations. Within the last two years he had entered into partnership with an old-established practitioner, a surgeon in the adjoining town, and there being between his family and this gentleman a long-tried friendship, they were enabled to conduct matters in a peaceful and profitable manner. His position being thus comparatively secure, Walter had obtained the consent of Mr. Vincent, and the marriage was to take place in a few days; thus before them seemed a future of unclouded happiness.

Some writers possess the peculiar tact of drawing interest from the dullest of all dull things, a truly English modern genteel party: they will tell you about the dances, repeat to you the vapid, unmeaning, envious, and hypercritical small-talk, describe the furniture with all the care of an auctioneer's inventory, and the silks, satins, bows, ribbons, flowers, jewellery, and even the very boots and shoes serve as matter for your regular bookmaker to dish up for the edification of the reader, I have not the will, nor do I possess the power, to enter into such minutiæ. The chilling genteel parties of your very genteel people, and your fashionable balls, are to me the greatest species of boredom the world can inflict me with. I am no recluse, nor am I uncharitable in saying this, but I hate most cordially anything where the artifical and the false are predominant. As a proof of good will towards real enjoyment I prefer a good old hard-working country dance to all the stiff, formal, figurative quadrilles that were ever invented. Although a young man, above even a country dance I prefer a good romp, as if the days of my birchdom and boyhood had not passed away. I love to hear the lungs expanding in the joyous laugh, without entailing on their owner the unenviable title of an "uncultivated bear."

Now, Mr. Vincent had deemed it necessary for the welfare of his daughters to succumb to modern taste and become a genteel man; this was, therefore, a genteel party. I have called them merry—so they were after a fashion, but it was a sort of consumptive mirth, until Walter entered: his presence was welcomed by one and all. The moment he left the room it was like a cloud falling over the assembly—he returned, and all was light again. Why was this? Simply because he had the power and audacity to break through the formality and frigidity that surrounded him. Against their own sense of what was or was not "right and proper," people were made to laugh, and the natural instincts of their nature were brought forth. In others such infringements might not have been received; in him there was a gentlemanly style which made them irresistible. At length the time arrived for all parties to separate, and the guests had all departed, save and except one gentleman who lingered beneath the porch of the cottage door, in close conversation with a lady, whilst another forlorn individual sat on the garden gate idly swinging his legs and whistling. The gentleman in the first and decidedly most agreable position was Walter, and the lady Kate Vincent, whilst the friend on the gate was waiting to accompany Walter home, as they lived within a few doors of each other. "Ah!" thought the former, "what a lucky rascal he is—what a silver lining in his life-cloud is this pretty and amiable girl. And there he stands with his arm round her waist, their heads almost touching; confound it, it is enough to make a fellow wild—I can't look any longer;" so he very wisely turned away, but was soon interrupted in his reverie by a merry "whoop" at his side, from Walter, and together they started on their homeward journey.

"Well," said his friend, "you are a pretty fellow to keep me waiting all this while—half-an-hour if it is a minute. The next time you have a little matter of that kind to settle I shall provide myself with a nightcap, and take a snooze under the hedge."

"Well, old fellow," replied Walter, "I am very sorry, but could not help it; it may have appeared long to you, having nothing else but the moon to look at, but you see I had a pair of bright eyes which, decidedly for us mortals, hath a stronger magnetic influence than that elderly, though much respected lady. Upon my life, to me it scarcely seemed a minute.

"Very likely!—hours are minutes, I know, when a pretty girl is in the field. You are a happy dog. I get no such opportunities, although I have been on the look-out since I was thirteen years old; if I ever do succeed I'll punish the unlucky wight I have for a companion as you do me."

"Do, do; you have my full permission—take ample vengeance on him. And now let us change the subject. Bob, tip us a stave. 'Woman, dear woman! the charm of our life!—' Confound it! when I attempt to sing, I generally break down, though that has been my crack song for the last ten years. Sing something with a rattling chorus; I'll join you in that, for I have capital lungs, and I feel I must make a row of some kind." Suiting the humour of the moment, his friend commenced, but had scarcely finished a verse when he was interrupted by Walter.

"Wait a bit, Bob; I am just thinking—I can scarcely believe in a few days I shall be a married man. I cannot realize the happiness some how or other. What a dence of a world this is! We are always wanting something, which we no sooner get than we are striving after something else—and so we go on from year's end to year's end.

"I beg your pardon, Walter, that is certainly not the case with me. I made a full stop at the first something, and there I have stuck ever since."

"Look there!" said Walter, abruptly halting, and pointing towards the sky.

"What is the matter?" asked his friend.

"A shooting star; did you not see it?"

"Well, what of that? Do you suppose I have never seen one before?"

"If anybody lives there it must decidedly be uncomfortable," said Walter, especially after a good dinner. It strikes me that remark is somewhat profane, but never mind, I only wish I was there, or up in the moon, I think that would be the best place!"

"Then, why in the name of conscience don't you mount on a birch broom, like Mother Goose, and go up there, or else invent some patent ærial machine, only take care you don't make a mess of it, as somebody did of his wings in Rasselas."

"I know you only laugh at me, and really that is what I deserve, for I am always bothering my head about a future that must ever in this life remain a mystery, Fire away, Bob, let us have the other verses of that song."

With that, his friend commenced again. Walter

Worthington joined in, and their voices broke upon the silent streets of the little town as they entered it with song and laughter, occasionally, I have no doubt, startling some of the "snoring citizens," who, waking in drowsy wonder, listened, then cursing the cause, turned over once more, and drawing the clothes still closer round them, mounted again on the shadowy wings of dreamland. At length they arrived at an exceedingly nice house, with that air of staid respectability about it peculiar to professional men, especially doctors. It was Walter's home. They paused at it just as two o'clock chimed forth from the old gray turret of the parish church.

"Good night! or rather, good morning!" said Walter. What a lovely night it is, almost too lovely for sleep. Talking of sleep, what is it Byron says?—

"'Death, so call'd, is a thing that makes men weep,
And yet a third of life is passed in sleep.'

"Not a bad idea that!"

"Yet remember there is a vast deal of difference, Walter, between the two; our every day is a sleep of exhaustion; the sleep of death is a sleep of eternity."

"And so much the better, when you get tired of life; but I am not going to argue the matter with you. Good night, old fellow!"

"Good night! See you to-morrow, Walter?"

"All right," cried Worthington, entering his house, and his friend turned up the street whistling and thinking at the same time, "what a happy fellow he must be, he hasn't a care. I do not envy him, but I wish myself in his shoes."

Morning dawned, a bright and glorious morning; the lark was upon the wing carolling a thrilling welcome to the king of light. From each tree and bush feathered songsters greeted the early rays; the flowers opened their petals to bask in sunshine, and shook off the dewy tears of night, the bee humming in gladness sought the honey-cup; the poor, ill-paid yet contented husbandman rose from his humble lair and whistled merrily as he sought the fields; even the wretched half-starved unowned mendicant dog stretched himself, and rising from his airy lodgings on the door step wagged his tail, and with renewed vigour sought a breakfast amongst the garbage of the gutters.

At the door of Walter Worthington's house a decently-dressed mechanic was knocking, and from the violence of his efforts he had seemingly been so engaged for some time. Presently, a window on the top floor opened and a head was thrust out, evidently belonging to a young fellow only half awake. "Steady, there, old chap!" cried the head, "you'll knock the door down, if you go on that way. What's the row?"

"Is Mr. Saunders at home?" asked the stranger, in an agitated voice.

"No, he doesn't live here; he is out of town."

"What shall I do?" murmured the man—"What a pity!"

"Now then, old cock, I am not going to stay here, catching cold; what do you want?"

"Is Mr. Worthington at home?" asked the man.

"I believe he is; if he isn't he ought to be. Who has the stomach-ache?"

"My wife, sir, is very ill, very ill indeed!" said the man.

"Why couldn't you say so before? Who is your wife?"

"Mrs. Larkins—the master has been attending on her before."

"Why don't you tell me something new?" facetiously replied the young fellow at the window, who was the articled assistant. "All right; I'll shake Mr. Worthington up. He'll be at your house in a crack!"

"Thank you, sir," said the man, who with hasty steps retraced his path home to rouse the sinking energies of his suffering wife with the promise of approaching medical aid. The assistant, of course, not in the least hurrying himself, pulled on his clothes and went downstairs to the room of Worthington. He knocked several times, but receiving no reply at length cautiously opened the door and entered. The blinds of the windows had not been drawn down, so that the morning sun with unobstructed brilliancy shone into the room, and fell upon the form of the sleeper as he lay in bed, with his face from the door. On a chair were carelessly thrown the clothes he had worn the night before, and on a small round table, which had been moved to the side of the bed, stood an empty ale bottle, a tumbler with a few dregs of beer at the bottom, and by the side of the tumbler a small phial. The right arm and hand of Worthington lay exposed upon the coverlid, whilst between the fingers he held a half-smoked cigar, of which the room smelt strongly, and the ashes were scattered on the bed. "Oh! that is the little game," muttered the assistant, "so you were out on the spree last night, governor, were you, and you finished up when you got home. What a devil of a sleep he must be in!—I'll shake him up." He approached the bed and took the sleeper's hand. The very touch blanched his face and made him tremble, he almost fell to the ground, and in doing so gave an impetus to the body of Walter, turning it over facing him—a corpse! The face rested full within the glare of sunshine, the eyes were unnaturally dilated, the pupil hardly visible, the features were firmly set, cold and marble-like, the mouth being slightly drawn down. Notwithstanding all this, divesting the face of its horrors, there was a peculiarly calm expression ; whilst the hair, short, curly and jet black, contrasting with the alabaster of the skin, added to the strangeness of the spectacle. The assistant for a moment stood dumb with fear, unable even to articulate. On his senses returning he at once went to the table, and took up the phial. It was labelled " Poison," and on a piece of paper at its side was written, " One more pull at the cigar, and then——" This broke the spell, for rushing through the house, he made it resound with his cries.

By the aid of poison, thus calmly and deliberately, in the midst of health, wealth, and every blessing the heart could apparently wish for, without reason assigned, or a word of regret to the young, loving and innocent girl whom he had parted from but a few hours back, had Walter Worthington dared that death against which

" There is a prohibition so divine,
It cravens my weak hand."

PRIDE:

A FASHIONABLE WATERING PLACE.

"We laugh heartily to see a whole flock of sheep jump because one did so; might not one imagine that superior beings do the same by us, and for exactly the same reason?"

GREVILLE.

Fashion, a word which knaves and fools may use
Their knavery and folly to excuse.

CHURCHILL.

Off the southern coast of England there is a watering place, celebrated as holding the first rank for its aristocratical pretentions, and, as must of necessity follow, its exclusiveness. In the last respect its society forms a striking example of this peculiar and unamiable characteristic of the English, in contradistinction to our more lively and agreeable continental neighbours. Woe to the male or female bold enough to attempt breaking through the stalactitic orbit surrounding this hemisphere of stars and planets of superior humanity (?) unless bearing with them a passport guaranteeing, his or her patrician blood back to the fourth and fifth generation. Though a being moulded in a less pretentious clay, it has been my lot to pass one or two of the fashionable months for several seasons here; and being naturally of a contented disposition, regarding little the buzzers or gadflies of our every-day life, I have contrived to enjoy myself from several reasons—firstly, because I am able to boast of a very pleasant circle of friends; secondly, I love to explore the beautiful environs; and thirdly, I find amusement in loitering along the shore, when the tide is out, to examine the little translucid pools (after the manner of tourists in general) to find I can't exactly say what, or still better to persuade myself I am a great deal wiser than people in general, and fully calculated to philosophize over the folly and vanity of a community who ought, by right of their education and position, to set a better example than they generally do—folly which the fashion and ambition of lionizing may sanction in their minds, but which even womanly delicacy should shrink from, and common sense must repudiate.

The town of (we must give it a name—Pride will do as well as any other) is certainly in itself very attractive, possessing a very lengthy and imposing pier, an excellent esplanade, great cleanliness, and capital bathing. You have but to mount one of the coaches (four-horse coaches too) though not the good old rattling, dust-besmothering mails of other days, but their younger sons—chips of the old block—to be respected for their novelty; they start at short intervals during the day, and in the course of half an hour, or so, you will be the delighted spectator of as fine wooded and undulating or bold and romantic scenery, as may be found enclosed within the white cliffs of this favoured land. There is a certain amount of homogeneousness in the peculiarities of all English watering places—more or less Cockneyism pervades everything—and here, too, as elsewhere. The tradespeople make the most of their harvest season by imposing on your good nature and your pocket to the best of their ability—ape the vices instead of the virtues of their betters; hotel touters and Bath chairmen (a numerous class here) worry you, pier proprietors make you pay well, German bandsmen blow away from morning until night, acrobats make your blood run cold by their horrible contortions, niggers make bad puns, and your eyes are in danger of being knocked out by gentlemen for everlasting looking through telescopes, young ladies are ducked by blue-serged matrons, naughty little boys and girls object to their threatened ablutions, despite the insinuating—"Will 'em have a little swim—a rosy-posy?" or other jargon familiar to us in our juvenile days, young gentlemen (unripe mushrooms) exhibit themselves to the best or worst advantage in hats, caps, and head gears of all sorts, colours, and denominations, with neck-circumventing collars, and garments as draft-boardy, stripe-impounding, or Neptune-like imposing as the most valued heart could wish. Thus far we recognise the spirit of Cockneyism in Pride; but, if I may be allowed the opinion, for the general costume and free and easy conduct of the ladies, Pride stands alone in its glory or its extravagance. Crinolines of the most outrageous dimensions impose the necessity of keeping a respectful distance; here waists are contorted to unnatural and most injurious proportions; boots of all colours of the rainbow—to quote Sir John Suckling—

> "Like little mice,
> Steal gently in and out."

Though, by-the-bye, this very sweet similie will hardly hold good with the young Countess of P—, who, during her visit here, took to first-rate regalias and Wellingtons. Here dresses are festooned like the valances of our drawing-room window curtains. Jackets are worn, as near as it is possible to have them, resembling the masculine cut, and it becomes fashionable to thrust the little delicate, jewelled ungloved hands in the side-pockets of their jackets, which, with an elaborately feathered wide-awake, cocked on one side, gives a decided *negligée* and saucy expression. It is not by any means an uncommon occurrence to find yourself rudely impelled off the pavement by half-a-dozen gentlemen in yachting costume, forming the body-guard round a single lady; thus they perambulate the streets and accompany her to the shops, laughing and loudly talking, more like rude and boisterous children just let out of school than educated people. Heaven help the character of any respectable tradesman's daughter who would dare be guilty of indiscretion that here may be daily seen enacted by these fair members of the highest households of this and other countries. The most accomplished flirt—she who can the most easily assume the masculine gender—would appear to be the most admired. I am not like the fox; in fact I have a most decided antipathy to that animal, who called the grapes sour because they were beyond his reach. I can admire—and do admire—many things in the position of the fox, but I hate extremes in the fair sex; it is degrading to them, as any outrage upon that graceful and modest deportment we look for must of necessity be. Would it were possible that the following delightful lines of the poet Rowe could be written indelibly in their hearts and minds:—

> "The bloom of op'ning flowers, unsullied beauty,
> Softness, and *sweetest innocence* she wears,
> And looks like nature in the world's first spring."

Or turning to the pages of Ben Jonson's "Silent Woman," first acted in 1609, there is a verse of a madrigal singularly appropos to the subject, and happy in its quaintness—

> "Give me a look, give me a face,
> That makes simplicitie a grace;
> Robes loosely flowing, haire as free:
> Such sweet neglect more taketh me
> Than all the adulteries of art,
> That strike mine eyes, but not my heart."

But enough of this moralizing, let us take a peep at one or two of the lions I have had the gratification—that is not the word, but let it pass—of seeing here. First of the list stands Mr. Fussabout Nancy. This gentleman is a resident, remarkable in his appearance only, for a moderately good looking face, minus expression, a bandbox exactness of costume, his penchant for light kid gloves, and the everlasting glass in his eye, which people (good-natured ones, of course,) say he even sleeps with. This gentleman is the Beau Nash, or Beau Brummel of Pride, without their liberality, he belongs to that order of the biped tribe denominated "ladies' men!" insipid and lackadaisical members of the human family. No resident or visitor of his "set" deems her dress worthy of wearing, without the ordeal of his critical eye. He is the choice chaperon to the linen-drapers, the prime disposer of ribbonds, laces, and knicknacks. A fancy fair is his element, he is the very spirit of the sales and the small-talk, the arranger of the stalls, the pincushions, the anti-Macassors, and the patchwork. Formerly one of the oldest and most respected inhabitants of Pride, an inhabitant and householder when Pride was little better than a fishing village, and you had to play at "pig-a-back" with boatmen to get on shore—then and for years this gentleman gave four balls during the season. Mr. Nancy found out he could do it cheaper—*six shillings* a ticket, or a guinea for the four, including coffee and negus, *was too much*. Shade of Beau Nash, what do you say to this? So Mr. Nancy hired the rooms over a pastry-cook's shop, he being *pro tem.* the Baron Nathan of each occasion, and ladies of title, and gentlemen with high-sounding names, were much happier in dancing and making merry sixpence a-head cheaper. I hear he has even improved upon this, and established for the winter months a *shilling hop*, once a week. Here's economy! Here's an example for your Chancellor of the Exchequer! Now that private theatricals are the rage, he is considered a most accomplished actor. Other people, who make it their profession, take years of hard work to learn the art, with credit to themselves, and these too often are far from achieving their end; but our gentlemen amateurs are all actors in their own conceit, they are born so, it comes intuitively to them, I suppose they take in the knowledge with their mother's milk. Nancy, of course, had the entire management of all such displays in his aristocratic circle. I can bear witness that he is an original actor, having had the honour of seeing him play a poor Corsican peasant, dressed in an elaborately-brocaded costume, a sort of brigand chief highly coloured, in fact, as the boys say, " all kivered in gold and silver ;" and this artistic and peasant-like costume was rendered still more striking by the glass in his eye. I suppose, however, it was correct, judging from the hearty congratulations of the audience. We may conceive the peasants in Corsica to be a vastly different race to the peasants in England, as passing by the gaudy apparel,—some of our clodpoles would look rather uncomfortable digging up potatoes, or feeding pigs as they quizzed through the last appendage.

A few winters ago, the quiet inhabitants were startled from their propriety, and the cheering propensities of the little boys rose to an alarming pitch by the introduction of a sledge *à la* Russ, driven by Mr. Nancy to the accompaniment of numerous bells. The ladies required a novelty, the sledge was the very thing, and for several mornings Fussabout was in the seventh heaven of delight in finding himself "the observed of all observers." By turns, he gave the fair creatures a drive up one street and down another, when, alas! for poor human ambition, on the occasion of the youngest daughter of Lady S—— accompanying him, the sledge upset, and the occupiers were ruthlessly pitched on to the snow, to the infinite amusement of the little boys, who greeted the event with vociferous cheers. I need scarcely add, the sledge, the cause of this dire calamity, was ever afterwards regarded with the utmost abhorrence. Enough of this gentleman, let us introduce a second lion, or rather lioness. The Honourable Mrs. T—— and her two daughters, in consequence of their very high connections, and their association with royalty, were objects of great envy, emulation, and admiration. There resided at Pride a weather-beaten old naval half-pay captain, whom we will call Twiddle. Report declared him rich, and living for some years separated from his better-half (or worse, as it would seem,) custom declared him a bachelor. Although a gentleman in the common acceptation of the word, he did not belong to the planetary system of Pride: he was, therefore, rather tolerated than received, yet strange to relate, the honourable Mrs. T. at once discovered in him great virtues, took compassion on his lonely situation, and her daughters, "those sweet girls," attended the old gentleman out for his airings; sometimes they playfully called him "papa," then the old man's eyes twinkled with gratification, not that the honourable Mrs. T. augured anything from this. At church it was quite delicious to observe the attention he received. He hired a pew on purpose that the ladies might attend him. He sat between the two "dear girls," who by turns found him the hymn, or the page in the book of prayers, presenting it to him with an innocent smile, acknowledged by the old gentleman with a grin and a nod, whilst the mama looked at first one and then the other, as much as to say, "are they not darlings? You must love and remember them." And did Twiddle "remember" when he died?—No! Hear it, and blush for him, the monster! He was smiled upon in vain—he left his money to his widow. The honourable lady and her two daughters were also frequent visitors to the poor; they descended from the pinnacle of their grandeur to enter the humble cottage, and they filled, not the stomachs, but the heads of the poor with good advice: their theme was *contentment*, whilst the half-starved wretches listening to them only pondered how much bread their silks, their satins, and their jewellery would purchase. They told these people of the martyrs, and chided them if they complained: "it was wicked;" above all they must attend regularly at church. If they ventured a remonstrance "they had nothing to go decent in." (And, reader, they are decent men and women in Pride—you see no rags and filth on their bodies—think of this, poor people of Manchester, Sheffield, Leeds, Bristol, London, and a thousand other places. We will excuse the dirt of industry, but we cannot excuse the rags of indolence.) Then would the Christian visitors, like so many other Christian visitors, shut up the Holy Book which teaches patience, and despite their own doctrines on that score, declare them at once incorrigibles, leaving them in anger to their hunger and their nakedness.

Pride was in a state of great excitement one morning by the honourable Mrs. T—'s carrying a smoking jug of broth through the streets to a poor and talented artist, dying of consumption! "What an example!"—and ladies with jugs of broth became the fashion. The broth, doubtless, was acceptable, but why make charity the vehicle for display? Byron says:—

> "The drying up a single tear has more
> Of honest fame than shedding seas of gore."

A beautiful sentiment, expressed in a beautiful couplet; but let the tear be dried in secret. Then we have the virtue of charity—the true principle, and not without. The reward of charity should alone rest in an approving conscience. One more lion, and I have done. Who has not heard of the great real, original, and highly-coloured lion-hunter, in comparison with whom Van Hamburgh or the late Mr. Carter sink into insignificance—whose wondrous exploits beneath the burning sun of Africa, and "hair-breadth 'scapes i' the imminent deadly breach" have made the hair upon every school-boy's hair stand up "like quills upon the fretful porcupine." Young ladies, and old ones, regard him with delight and awe, and muttered exclamations are heard—"Ah, my dear, he is something like a man!" Heedless of the excitement he creates, he walks down the middle of the road—the road, mind. He has been used to deserts, and could he, like other men, confine himself to the pavement? How finely is his tall and manly figure developed by that Highland costume, and what a peculiar expression is given to his face by his hair being worn in a net behind. There's something strikingly original about this; and then his beard—look at it with envy, you beardless youths. What is it he bears in his hand, tied up in a cloth? Go with him to the end of the pier and you will see. It is his dinner. Think of this, ye uninitiated, in the peculiarities of lion-hunters when they get into civilized society. You see, their old habits cling to them—not that he in the deserts had the pier steps to sit on and eat his dinner; but he may now imagine it a rock—a fallen tree—and the waters of the Sound, now gently irrigating the wooden supports, the sand of the desert. There is a great deal in imagination; the colour is somewhat different—one is a liquid, the other a solid—one is at rest, the other in motion; but, gentle reader, in the wild flights of the ideal, imagination strides over worse difficulties than these. A great nautical hero, and pet with the playgoing public, on the eve of his execution informs a spasmodic young lady with a pale face, wild, staring eyes, and dishevelled hair (the usual concomitants of a breaking heart), that "many a summer's day aboard I've lain in the top and looked at these few leaves until I saw green meadows in the salt sea, and heard the bleating of the sheep." Then why should not the bold lion-hunter sit on the steps of Pride pier, spread his handkerchief on his knees, demolish the contents of his basin, and see the African desert "in the salt sea," minus the sheep? However, one thing is certain—the ladies regarded him as something particularly interesting—the very food that he ate was worthy of remark. Such an example being set, in the rage for emulating the out-of-the-way and ridiculous, I much wondered at it not being more generally adopted, as I expected to find Pride pier turned into a monster cook's-shop, bearing at its head the very apropos sign of "Restaurent de la Folie."

Should this sketch catch the eye of any moderately good-looking curate, afflicted with the dire and common complaint of poverty, and should he be willing to swallow the matrimonial pill, he may in Pride find an effectual and speedy cure. Hitherto its effects may be guaranteed on high authority; the church at which he officiates will become the favoured resort for the time being, of all the young unmarried and disengaged ladies. In their attentions he will find them equal, if not superior, to the community of another district I am acquainted with, where the descendants of Eve presented their pastor with a dozen shirts of the finest fabric (not that I believe he was short of linen at the time, though many curates are, with shame be it written,) each shirt bearing his name, beautifully wrought, with the raven chesnut or Madonna hairs abstracted from their pretty heads. On one occasion a reverend gentleman came to Pride, of the confirmed bachelor school, and being delighted with the general attention of the female portion of his congregation, and desirous to set any religious doubts they might have at rest, he (poor innocent!) had a box fixed in the lobby to receive communications on the subject. What a chance. They were all overwhelmed with doubts—not religious, but doubts he had not the courage to answer. The letter-box was removed, and the dear doubting creatures continued to doubt in secret. If you are poor, the case may be different: you might be inclined to solve the doubts of one of their number, as others have done, by propounding the desperate query which has proved the turning point of joy or sorrow to us and our forefathers since the days of Adam.

I shall conclude this sketch with an anecdote, proving that not only are the coaches here to be respected as the last remaining type of a vehicle, rendered dear to us by how many a familiar tale of our fathers and our grandfathers, but that the coachmen also retain some portion of the hereditary mantle of wit, ascribed to the jolly old fellows forming that class in days gone by. Mr. P——, a gentleman, and a very proud one in his way, kept a donkey chaise, with just room for "one inside," and all hours of the day he was to be seen walking by its side, as it slowly and surely conveyed his spouse for her airings. They were passing up a narrow road leading out of Pride, when, to the horror of the lady and the anger of her lord, a four-horse coach brought them to a stand. Mr. P—— insisted on the coachman driving into the hedge, at the risk of the passengers' necks, and that individual suggested the donkey chaise should return.

Argument on both sides being useless, the coachman gave his horses the whip, and the coach passed on at the imminent risk of Mrs. P—— and the donkey, as it was, breaking her parasol and frightening her out of her wits. It would be difficult to describe the rage of the pompous Mr. P——, who insisted on the coachman's descending from his exalted position and offering an ample apology for the insult. The coachman not seeing the necessity for such a course, and knowing the old man's peculiarities, rose from his box and thus addressed his passengers—" Ladies and gentlemen, I appeals to you if it's the sort of thing, in a civilized country, for a gent who is a-driving a four-in-hand to demean himself by descending from his box to apologize to another gent who is only a donkey driver." " Ha! ha! ha!" roared the passengers—crack sounded the whip, and " d—n his impudence," shouted the discomfited Mr. P——

THE JOLLY GOOD FELLOW.

"How like a younker, or a prodigal,
The scarfed bark puts from her native bay
Hugged and embraced by the strumpet wind!
How like the prodigal doth she return,
With over-weather'd ribs, and niggard
Lean, rent, and beggar'd."

SHAKESPEARE.

"Pain may be said to follow pleasure as its shadow."

COLTON.

"BROTHER BUFFS—I rise on this here most momentous occasion to propose the health of a Jolly Good Fellow! When I says a Jolly Good Fellow, I don't think many of you had need to be told I alludes to our noble Primo of the most Royal Order of Antediluvian Buffaloes, who sits as our chairman—(cheers)—and who has kept the game alive with all harmony and good feeling on this occasion, when we have met together to celebrate the annual dinner of our most ancient, glorious and noble order!—(loud cheers, with a pewter pot and tumbler accompaniment.) And here's a hand which afore it would refuse *him* a five-pun' note, when it had one to share, would cut off itself from my body, just as soon as it would knock down a bul-lock with one blow!—(vehement cheering.) I need say no more but to call upon you as gents and thorough-tried Buffs, to do justice to the toast, accompanying it with the usual honours up-standing, all on you!" Now, when it is understood that the Buffaloes had been doing nothing else but draining bumpers for seven hours, it is a conclusion which I should think may easily be arrived at, that to "up-stand" was not so easy of accomplishment as might at first appear. It was some time, therefore, before the company stood on their legs, and with stupid expressionless grins, and beery, bloated faces, awaited the signal to explode. It came at length, and as is usual on such occasions, it was responded to with a roar resembling the sudden explosion of a suppressed volcano, without a dozen of the boisterous revellers clearly understanding for what purpose they had been induced to make so much noise. Upon a slight cessation for the purpose of taking breath, and giving time for the neighbours in the adjoining houses to hear themselves curse, "a little one in for Mrs. Thompson and the little Thompsons," was suggested by Mr. Drinkwell, the master butcher, the same person who had previously spoken, as may be inferred from the touching and elegant bullock simile, who likewise rejoiced in the distinction of being a "Kangaroo," a particulur species of official attached to the Buffalo order. His last request was responded to by another outburst, and then the noble members resumed their seats, and a call for the chair was raised, when not the chair, but the chairman was seen to rise from his seat, his face and figure looming through the oppressive tobacco and gin and fog atmosphere; whilst he is perpetrating the usual "hem-s" and "ha-s," let us turn for a moment, gentle reader, to gossip over the society into which I have so abruptly introduced you. I think I hear you inquire—"but who the deuce are the Buffaloes?" All I can say is, they are not quadrupeds but bipeds, belonging to a society well known through the northern part of England, denominated "The Antediluvian Buffaloes," who meet every Sunday evening on an entirely exclusive principle, for the purpose of smoking "weed" and drinking "gatter." You will understand these are strictly classical names, insisted on by the rules of the society to signify tobacco and beer.

The order, I believe, in its records, dates its origin from the earliest period of Christianity, and further affirms William the Conqueror was enrolled a member, but as history fails to tell us that the great Norman warrior was addicted to "long clays" and "heavy wet" whilst meditating on the invasion of England, and further, as the said luxuries were not known for some centuries after, we are compelled to doubt the truth of the assertion. The place of meeting on the present occasion was the large room of the "Rose and Crown," a favourite place of resort for the smoke-pipe, gossipping part of the male community of Guzzleton, a county town in the north of England.

Having explained thus far, we will return to the individual commonly known as Bob Thompson, whom we so unceremoniously left "standing on his legs," and introduce him with due form.

Amongst his associates he was generally spoken of as "The Jolly Good Fellow." His father, by dint of honest industry and strict integrity, had risen from the humble calling of a bricklayer's labourer to that of a respectable master builder; but as is too often the case, when years of unremitting toil and care gain for its victim comparative independence, and comfort, the die is cast, the ordination is sent forth, and he is shifted from off the stage, where he has so faithfully played his part, leaving to others the enjoyment resulting from his anxiety and labour. Thus was it with him; and at five-and-twenty Robert Thompson found himself the proud possessor of what—though to the "silver-spooned" part of creation might be accounted a trifle—to a man of humbler pretensions was a considerable sum, sufficient to have enabled him, in the ten years transpiring since his father's death, had he possessed only a reasonable amount of common sense and assiduity, to have accounted himself in a substantially respectable and even wealthy position. But he had yet to learn the truth of Colton's moral precept, "The seeds of repentance are sown in youth by pleasure, but the harvest is reaped in age by pain," a truth how dearly purchased we have opportunities of learning every hour of our life. The honest, humble-hearted old man, just previous to his death, called his son to his bedside, and thus addressed him—"Robert, thy father was turned upon the streets an orphan, without a single friend in the wide world, but with a hopeful heart, which bore him up many a time when food was scarce and he felt himsel a stumbling from the path of Christ. It were my hope now that I were comfortable like, to enjoy the bit o' money I ha' scraped together —but the will o' the Almighty be done. Thee as the privilege given thee, lad, which I am denied; and now listen to my last words:—Make others respect thee by larning to respect thyself. Be honest and just in all thy dealings, and faithfully fulfil thy stewardship. Do this, or thy old father's bones will ne'er lay quiet in his grave, but in the days of thy sorrow and thy shame his spirit shall be thy accuser." The old man's fears proved only too true, for in the chair of honour at the ale-house, and in the drunken orgies of its frequenters, his son found his only ambition, whilst the trust of his stewardship was wasted in the stomachs of his selfish, sottish, and treacherous companions. Now, as he stood and gazed around with bloated face and eyes, in which drunkenness, pride, and misguided good-nature commingled—whilst the cheers of the half-stupid crew surrounding him still rang in his ears, Napoleon himself, when for the first time he felt the golden badge of sovereignty, could not, in gratified ambition, have experienced a stronger pleasure. The speech in which he returned thanks consisted of the usual amount of nonsense, tautology, and fulsome unmeaning flattery. Of course "the honour was little expected," although the present acknowledgment had been the theme of consideration for the last six months; and as the reader will be perfectly well aware, it was "the proudest moment of his life." We need, therefore, only repeat the concluding part, which ran somewhat thus—"I will only say, I hope the harmony of this evening may continue until we are all in as jolly a state as the jolliest heart could wish: and again let me thank you, gents all, and brother Buffs, for the kind and feeling manner in which you have *drunk my wife* and my little ones. Ah! them's a sacred trust, gentlemen. ("Hear, hear," from Mr. Stubbs, a journeyman tailor with ten). A very sacred trust, gents. My friend Mr. Stubbs says hear! hear! and he feels like a father. I shall tell my wife of the great honour you have done her and her children, that she may share with me in the pride and satisfaction I feel on this most momentous occasion. (Cheers.) Gents, I drinks to you all. I hope you will all live long to enjoy the harmony and brotherly love of the Antediluvian Buffaloes, and may we stand up like men when our country calls upon us, and never disgrace—

> "The flag that's braved a thousand years
> The battle and the breeze"—

which last sentiment was received with loud and long-continued cheering. The harmony of the evening was now continued by Mr. Pottle, a light-haired young man, rejoicing in the occupation of barber's assistant, who sang with great gusto that plaintive and antiquated ballad of "The Soldier's Tear," commencing—

> "Upon the hill he turned," &c.

which was melodized by the aspiring hair-dresser

to the tune of "With a helmet on his brow," &c., concluding each verse with a general chorus of—

> " And he dropp'd a tear my boys,
> And he dropp'd a tear my boys,
> And the soldier leant upon his sword,
> And he dropp'd a tear my boys !"

This being totally at variance with the correct version was correspondingly well received by his intellectual audience. After him came Mr. Snipyard, a journeyman tailor, the comic singer of the company, who dolled out a never-ending song, about "A slap-up four-and-nine," in the most melancholy manner imaginable, fancying himself extremely funny, but whose great achievement was the "Theatrical Barber," in which he was supposed to imitate many great actors, but the difference between each rested entirely in his own imagination, his auditors too often falling into the error of mistaking Macready for Buckstone, and Paul Bedford for Mr. C. Kean. At length, the company generally being too drunk to furnish the landlord with any more profit, were informed by that individual " he was sorry to disturb them, but it was getting late, and they mun go." The breaking up led to three times repeated parting cups, when the Antediluvian Buffaloes, Kangaroos and all, betook themselves as they were best able to their homes, the street gutters, or the station-house. As for Bob Thompson, he, accompanied by Mr. Drinkwell and another friend, wended his way up the street, singing " We won't go home till morning," or " Smilin' morn," having determined " to make a night of it," (it was now only three o'clock in the morning,) and from the fact of their being still able to speak, it is to be inferred they were not yet as "jolly" as the jolliest heart could wish.

Presto! change! I wave the scribbler's magic wand, rendering time or space immaterial, and transport you to a different scene. A few streets off from the " Rose and Crown " stood a moderate-sized dwelling, half-shop and half-house. Not wishing to enter by the front door, the visit being strictly private, let us go round to the back, and seeing a glimmering light through a dirty holland blind, we will unceremoniously enter the room. Its dimensions were small, its furniture old but tolerably good, portions of children's clothing and some few broken toys lay scattered about, whilst the remnants of a supper stood on the table. The candle had burnt down in the socket of what had once been a plated candlestick, and was now sputtering into life by fits and starts, struggling to maintain its existence. Strange and mysterious shadows fell from its lambent beam, and wandered or glided from floor to wall, and from wall to ceiling, and a few calcined cinders lay mouldering in the grate. In the angle of the wall sat a delicate, careworn woman, with hair untimely gray, whose low and monotonous lulling resembled the wailing of one who suffered pain, as she rocked the cradle at her feet, and bore another child across her knee, this was the only sound breaking through the stillness and midnight gloom. *One! two! three!* strikes by the old Dutch clock in the corner, when the woman paused, and lifted her languid eyes to its white shining face, then with a long-drawn sigh she sank back exhausted in her chair. God help her! poor soul! for sixteen long hours, ill and sick as she was, had this been her task, for both her children were suffering from childish malady, and for her there seemed no help but to "do and suffer."

Presently her eyes were again raised to the clock, and anon a scarcely discernible smile seemed to light up her face. It appeared as if the rude and gaudy representation of a rose had struck some sweetly vibrating chord of her neglected heart, for a gleam of brightness played for a moment about her blue sad-looking eyes, as if memory had wandered back, far back, from this narrow, lonely room, to bright summer fields and gay flowery hedgerows. It was so, for she murmured of them, and it was evident that ill-painted daub upon the old Dutch clock face was to her heart what a straw is to the last despairing yet hopeful fingers of the drowning man. It is often so in the hour of affliction and sorrow: the merest trifle may cause us to forget the dreary present, and, although but for a moment, give us a draught of joy, which the wealth of worlds can never otherwise restore.

Her reverie was at length interrupted by the arrival of her husband, Bob Thompson, accompanied by Drinkwell and another companion. No sooner were they seated than the "jolly good fellow" insisted on their "picking a bit," pointing to the supper on the table, urging his request by strong assurances of how heartily they were welcome. They took him at his word, and poor Mrs. Thompson saw the only remnants of food, preserved for herself and children on the morrow, quickly disappear. "What was she to do?" she asked herself over and over again, as mouthful after mouthful was passed into her husband's guests' capacious jaws. She knew too well no hope was left her from him; he had done no work lately, and the shilling or two he might still have would be reserved for the "Rose and Crown" on the morrow, for after a night's debauch it was customary to wind up on the following day. She did not like to speak, for "Robert would be angry;"

so she only sighed, placed spirits and pipes (articles always to be found in the jolly good fellow's house) before the trio, then stole silently to her bed with a child in either arm. The eldest she laid gently upon the pillow, whilst closer, and still closer to her bursting heart she pressed her baby, and into its unconscious ears she poured her sorrows. As the pillow grew damp with her tears, she thought of the wreck to which she had clung. It was not for herself she cared—selfishness found no room within her gentle heart—it was for her children, and the sinking vessel she had trusted to, that even while she wept, was steering safely and surely to the rock of destruction. Above other thoughts stood prominently forward a large, plain, red brick building, with all its attendant horrors of separation and loneliness in the midst of many—cold bare-looking walls, stony-hearted and meanly-pompous officials, coarse diet, and still coarser livery to denote the poor pauper in its wearer, and to tell the world England may give, charity may extend its hand upon this soil, but England likes to make its gifts known, and, trumpet-tongued, proclaim its generosity, as it holds up its victims to the derision and contempt, too often, of the rich and the thoughtless many, or their condescending pity. To this goal she felt she must at last come. It was the only retreat except the grave remaining for her in the dreary vista of future poverty and sorrow. And where was the cause of all this evil? Drinking in the room beneath, and believing himself to be, in the distorted vision of his maudlin brain, the happiest as well as the best of men, whilst his companions pledged him at his own expense, and sang—"For he's a jolly good fellow," until the power both of thought and speech became absorbed in the potent evanescent spirit of alcohol.

At length time, that sad betrayer of all our secrets and our crimes, whispered to the inhabitants of Guzzleton that Robert Thompson's affairs were not in the most flourishing condition; he owed nothing at the "Rose and Crown," for ready money was the rule there, but he owed a great deal elsewhere. Bit by bit, piece by piece, houses, furniture, even wearing appparel had vanished, till nothing was left to raise money upon. What was to be done? He did not think so much of the future of his wife and children as of his own declining popularity, for now he had no money to spend with his boon companions and gaslight acquaintances—they withdrew from his society. The chair of honour in the bar was no longer his special station; his health was no longer proposed and answered by enthusiastic greetings as of old; even his friend Drinkwell thought better than to cut off his hand sooner than to refuse a "fiver"—he kept it to button up his pockets with; further, he usurped the presidential chair at the jovial meetings. Robert Thompson now experienced what his wife and children had long felt—the want of the common necessaries of life; he had done so before but for the self-devotion, the patient, drudging love of the woman who could so uncomplainingly suffer, eking out a bare sufficiency to keep life and soul together, so that he might want for nothing.

In hearing this, I beg of you to remember she is only one stray leaf I have culled out of the thousands of patient, trusting hearts that lie scattered unknown and unpitied about the world, who whilst you read are pursuing their lonely, toilsome course, with that still, small earth-bound sepulchre for their only hope of refuge, above whose heads the bright green grass may wave, and modest daisy blush into life, whilst the stranger tramples its beauty and its freshness into dust, as theirs have been, all heedless of the only memorial which nature has planted above them. Join with me, reader, in saying "God bless them!" for if heaven in its all seeing mercy reserves a place for the humble, forgiving, and meek-hearted, these are the women deserving such distinction, above all other examples which the world can give.

The day at length arrived which saw him dragged to gaol, and not one hand was extended for the "jolly good fellow's" relief. Ten pounds would have averted this catastrophe, but he could not raise it, and his wife, who pleaded for him, was thrust from the door of the "Rose and Crown" like a beggar. On the night of his capture a convivial meeting was held there, when his misfortunes were freely discussed without a dissentient voice the landlord's opinion prevailed—"They all had seen for some time past how it would end. Thompson was a 'jolly good fellow,' but he must have been a fool to spend his money and neglect his business as he had done, when he had a wife and family at home to provide for." What a pity this was not *remembered* before! Thompson thought so as he lay, for the first time in his life, within the cold stone walls of a gaol, on a sharp winter's night, the night of his entrance. Sadly he threw himself upon his bed: his late experiences had somewhat dissipated the diseased shadow of pleasure which had so long filled his heart; the fever of his imagination, unaided by stimulants, had subsided into the dread certainty of reality. The last words of his poor old father now rang strangely in his ears, and thinking of him he fell into a painful slumber; then slowly through the darkness came the palsied figure of an aged man, clad in his grave clothes, whilst from his lips issued these texts from Proverbs :—

"As the bird by wandering, as the swallow by flying, so the curse causeless shall not come."

"As righteousness tendeth to life, so he that pursueth evil pursueth it to his own death."

"The eye that mocketh at his father, and despiseth to obey his mother, the ravens of the valley shall pick it out, and the young eagles shall eat it."

As he recognized the words so often quoted to him in his childhood, the "*Jolly Fellow*" started from his couch with the cold perspiration running down his forehead; he gazed around expecting to meet his father's face, but he was alone—alone in darkness! It would be useless longer to follow his career. He died in prison. Mrs. Thompson entered beneath the portals of that red brick building, the goal of her imagination, and found her fears but too sadly realised in the stern discomfort and cold apathy of all around; but amidst such experiences she soon passed away to the "land of shadows," where sorrow finds no room to enter. To a grave half-filled by human corruption, in a rude misshapen box, and without mourners, all that remained of her gentle spirit was hurried, and there amongst her pauper kindred left to rot, for as in life, so must the poor of charity mingle in death. The two children were in due time kicked upon the world, each in his turn to earn an epitaph culled from Beattie's poems :—

> " Check'd by the scoff of pride, by envy's frown,
> And poverty's unconquerable bar,
> In life's low vale remote he pined alone,
> Then dropt into the grave, unpitied and unknown !"

Such was the end of a " Jolly Good Fellow's" career, such the fate to which he doomed his wife and children: and such will be the result of the follies pursued by a thousand others like him, who, seeking to be "Jolly Good Fellows" in the mouths of the worthless, pursue a shadow which despoils them of the substance.

THE MISER'S DEATH.

Dying acursed—behold! the miser lay—
Night's deepest shadows hath obscur'd the day,
And phantoms wild and strange flit thro' the air,
Or haunt the walls, or on the miser stare.
The moon's pale light scarce penetrates the scene,
Whilst sordid misery but mocks HER beam;
Upon a couch outstretched, of dirty straw,
'Mid filth and rags offensive, on the floor
The wretch is laid; no fire to cheer the room;
His glaring eye-balls start from out the gloom;
And ever and anon is heard the groan
Of one *so* dying, suffering and lone.—
But see! He starts,—and wildly stretching out
His shrivell'd hands, he utters shout on shout—
"My gold!—my gold! Robbers! begone, forbear!"
And mocking echoes fill the stagnant air.—
As fiends or ghosts might add their yelling
From each crevice of the lonely dwelling!
A death-like silence follows the shrill cry,

When, lo! a whining howl is heard close by.
A half-starved dog leaps trembling on the bed,
O'er whose rough nature love, withal, had shed
The fondest throbbings of a faithful heart,
For HE it was that made the miser start—
Had lick'd his hand as he lay lost in thought,
Mourning the gold his avarice brought;
And fearing that *dread* hour when his dim sight
Would on it close in everlasting night.
He smooth'd the ONLY friend the world had left,
And half the gloom was by that dog bereft,
For in such hours of trembling and of pain,
Man will be *man*, despite of all, again—
Some touch of human feeling, past control,
Will vibrate softly o'er the hardened soul.
Together they had liv'd, and *dog* and *man*
Shar'd as by instinct, each the other's *ban*,
As cowering with fear, together laid,
They trembled at the sounds themselves had made.
So hours pass! when the miser starts again—
A fearful vision harrows up his brain:
Wildly he raves—he sees a fleshless form
(As from the *grave*, the long-decay'd were torn)—
Stand close beside him there; eyes it had not,
Yet still it gaz'd from where the eyes should rot—
The vacant sockets—but the teeth remain'd
To grin in triumph at the prize new gain'd.
A loathsome smell pervades, as of the mould,

When the wretch feels a hand, clammy and cold,
Slowly but surely creeping to his heart,
And numbing his flesh to the vital part.
With one despairing effort he doth rise,
To clasp his gold with a death-gripe he tries ;
But ere accomplish'd his lost soul hath fled,—
And back he falls upon his pallet—dead !

PAWSON AND BRAILSFORD, PRINTERS, HIGH STREET, SHEFFIELD.

www.ingramcontent.com/pod-product-compliance
Lightning Source LLC
Chambersburg PA
CBHW030826270326
41928CB00007B/909
9783744675321